# *DoctorBarre*

The First Academic Study of Barre

From the doctoral thesis

## THE HIGH BARRE:

*An Investigation of Barre for the Performing Arts in Higher Education*

Jill Rose Jacobs, PhD

DoctorBarre - The First Academic Study of Barre

By Jill Rose Jacobs, PhD

"Brava! … A gargantuan amount of blood, sweat and tears went into envisioning and putting together all of the findings into a comprehensive textbook that any serious practitioner in the health care and movement field will find invaluable."

— Sarita Allen, Ailey Extension Faculty and Founder of the Ailey Barre Program

"The Lotte Berk Method has enabled us to keep our strength and flexibility because of how we use our bodies. I am living proof at age 80 … This is the method for anti-aging."

— Lydia Bach, Owner and Founder, The Lotte Berk Method (US)

"An insightful analysis of an artform that is growing and evolving in the dance and fitness world."

— William Baugh, Performing Artist and Educator, *The Tina Turner Musical* (Hamburg, Germany)

"From filming Esther Fairfax's class in Hungerford, I can see the original Lotte Berk methods and how Jill is using those small [isometric] movements, constant [repetitious] small movements, in her own classes, then adding them to modern music, her own choice of music, and making them into a dance with choreography. I think it's really cool and really interesting the way that she's been able to modernize and fuse them together."

— Aimee Buckley, Owner, New Generation Film

"I've known Jill from when she was a professional dancer, dance professor, and later doctoral researcher. Jill has also always said, 'anyone can dance' and then made her students' lives better through her passion and knowledge of dance … I am proud to have participated in Jill's ICURe awarded *The High Barre* project in this thesis and fully support her research."

— Claudio Castiglioni, Co-founder and President, Beauty Thinkers

"Jill has achieved through her meticulous research a fascinating insight into the origins and development of Barre, as well as the sometime elusive history of both the person and the legacy of the legendary Lotte Berk. Here we have the inside scoop on what exactly makes Barre such an effective movement method and how we can hone and refine our own teaching."

— Anne Cheshire, Trauma Recovery Clinic, Edinburgh, Certified Barre Instructor by Lotte Berk

"Jill has been a support in my life since I first took her dance classes at NYU. At 260 lbs I couldn't really dance at all and she met me with love and understanding that I will never forget. Skip forward a decade … We spent three months building a new Barre format geared for men, though, of course, open to all! Jill is a constant inspiration and shining light in this world!"

> — Aaron Cooker, Actor, Musical Theatre, Opera, Currently Performing on Princess Cruises

"Written by internationally acclaimed Barre expert Jill Rose Jacobs, this critical research is a must-read for all Barre instructors, participants, and all health and wellness professionals looking to elevate and differentiate their programs and services with the real science behind Barre training. This highly detailed compilation includes the first in-depth exploration of the original Barre creator, Lotte Berk, and her innovative approach to movement. Ms Jacobs separates herself by including her years of research and documentation of the academic science behind this program and its physiological and health benefits. The first of its kind, I highly recommend this book!"

> — Carol Espel, Fitness and Program Director, Pritikin Longevity Center + Spa

"It's terrific, Jill, that you want to bring Lotte back to her rightful place, not in the fitness world, but in the performing arts. I'm so thrilled."

— Esther Fairfax, *An Interview with Esther Fairfax*, documentary, 2017

"Jill Rose Jacobs is not only a light and inspiration in the NYC and LA theater and film/tv community but a phenomenon in the dance and Barre worlds. A teacher and mentor, she has shown me that nothing is impossible and has encouraged me to push the boundaries of my artistry and craft. And THAT is precisely what she has done with her new work!"

> — Ta'Nika Renée Gibson, Actress (film/television), *Ain't Too Proud - The Life and Times of the Temptations*, Broadway, currently in the role of Diana Ross

"… clearly a significant contribution to knowledge in the field. The methodological innovations are also notable."

> — Dr. David Grant, Senior Lecturer, School of Creative Arts, Queen's University, Belfast; and Dr. Emma Redding, Head of Dance Science at Trinity Laban Conservatoire of Music and Dance – Doctoral Panelists

"It [Burlesque Barre] makes me feel like I'm living. It makes me feel younger. It makes me feel more elegant. It makes me feel more poised. It just helps me in all aspects of my life … It really improves posture, it improves deportment, and it also improves your mental state."

> — Lynsey Hakin, Image Consultant and Burlesque Barre Instructor

"Brava to Jill for this intensive research and data! FINALLY, there is documentation that factually clarifies the extensive history of the barre fitness world! A true barre fitness education on how this technique can support dancers and athletics."

> — Elisabeth Halfpapp, Barre Fitness Pioneer, Co-owner of CoreBarreFit

"I met Jill during her week in Hungerford while assisting Esther Fairfax with her teacher training. Jill's enthusiasm, knowledge, and skill in the Lotte Berk Method impressed both Esther and myself. In the five years since that time, Jill's integrity in her research, especially the historic backstory of Lotte Berk to explain the method's essence is amazing. Jill's thesis holds valuable information for every Barre enthusiast—it is the bible for the Barre instructor. I am honored to be included in Jill's research and highly recommend DoctorBarre!"

> — Bernadette Kenna, Former Assistant for Esther Fairfax; Owner of Love Lotte; Partner, The Lotte Berk Method

"The Lotte Berk Method and [Jill's] Barre methodology is really methodical and structured so that you can work all your body in a safe way."

> — Cindy Léonet, Mechanical Engineer

"I discovered Jill's classes as she was recommended to me by many other members at my club. I became a devout follower, attending multiple weekly classes over 5 years, often traveling around NYC to different locations where Jill was an instructor. Jill's barre classes were an elevating experience. Her class structure, choreography, and music contributed to my accomplishment and improvement. What's more, Jill inspired me to become a Barre instructor—she also trained and certified me. I recommend and endorse both Jill's classes and her study in the field of Barre."

> — Mathew Makings, Group Fitness Manager, Barre and Pilates Lead, Beverly Hills, CA

"I just love the class; I feel at my most alive!"

> — Dr. Amy Millar, Clinical Psychologist

"I was a runner for 25 years and, unfortunately, as I approached my 50th birthday, I had acquired a lot of injuries. I started Jill's Barre class in an effort to try and rehabilitate and ... I feel so much stronger and so much younger!"

— Anita O'Connor, Solicitor and Mother

"I would be a very introverted person, which is then kind of odd to go with dance and performance [the area of Jill's expertise] ... I was definitely helped by Jill's classes and Jill's energy ... From a medical perspective, people who have chronic pain and chronic mobility issues would be helped by having a form of exercise or form of movement that they are excited about, enjoy and want to go to ... [Jill's] Barre is that for me and is for so many other people."

— Dr. Ellen Pollheimer, Medical Doctor

"I certainly hadn't engaged in the idea of dance as having the different kinds of benefits both beyond movement but also psychologically and neurologically that she's [Jill] been able to point towards. It certainly has opened my eyes to what dance as an art form and as a mode of education can do ... So, all of this is pointing to a story in which dance is good not just for movement but also for motivation, for emotion, and sense of self because it has to do with the way that the brain and the body connect to each other, and they're not just distinct parts ... This may allow us to infer that in the kind of Barre training that Jill has developed, what may be going on in the brain because of the complexity of the movement and the skillful nature of it, is actually more advantageous than just moving for its own sake as a kind of physical activity."

— Dr. Matthew Rodger, Senior Lecturer, School of Psychology, Queen's University, Belfast

"Jill's technique is effective and useful both for an approach to dance and a routine suitable for treating and solving physical and psychological problems. Her exercises can be performed, with dedication and joy, by a large and differentiated audience, without any impediment even for a group characterized by advanced age. A new proposal which aims to increase well-being."

— Gianluca Schiavoni, Ballet Dancer and Choreographer, Teatro alla Scala

"She [Jill] works a lot with my students, teaching them body awareness, breathing, and how to think about the way they move when they're onstage ... They might be opera singers, also very traditional musicians, and some that might be more experimental, but they all have in common that they have to go onstage and use their bodies to speak to an audience."

— Dr. Franziska Schroeder, Professor for Music and Cultures, School of Arts, English and Languages, Queen's University, Belfast

"Jill combines historic activities with her own new work and she handles this very well by crediting the people that came up with the first parts of the work. This is a simple and straight forward approach and one that I thoroughly recommend ... Jill has developed Barre ... it's very good and she deserves recognition."

> — Jason Wiggins, Commercial Development Manager, Queen's University, Belfast

Dr Jill Rose Jacobs, author

# DoctorBarre

## The first academic study of Barre

Barre is a popular exercise regimen in the United States and United Kingdom that is currently understood as a fitness programme. This thesis proposes that Barre also may be understood as an arts-based programme, as it was originally intended by its founder, Lotte Berk, and highly suitable for the performing arts in higher education, with potential applications in the fields of medicine, rehabilitation, health & wellness, and education.

New information about Barre is presented through ethnographic interviews, critical analysis of the existing literature and media sources, and two case studies, offering a means by which to understand the origins and evolution of Barre and how the methodology can be tailored to benefit learners in varied environments.

Dr Matthew Rodger, Senior Lecturer in the School of Psychology at Queen's University, Belfast, notes in *The High Barre* video-documentary:

> I certainly hadn't engaged in the idea of dance as having the different kinds of benefits both beyond movement but also psychologically and neurologically that she's [Jill] has been able to point towards. It certainly has opened my eyes to what dance as an art form and as a mode of education can do . . . So, all of this is pointing to a story in which dance is good not just for movement but also for motivation, for emotion, and sense of self because it has to do with the way that the brain and the body connect to each other, and they're not just distinct parts… This may allow us to infer that in the kind of Barre training that Jill has developed, what may be going on in the brain because of the complexity of the movement and the skilful nature of it, is actually more advantageous than just moving for its own sake as a kind of physical activity.

In pursuit of deeper insight into the question of how Barre can be used and adapted to meet the needs of the performing arts in higher education and beyond, the researcher embarked on a mission to speak with experts and leaders in various fields, including medicine, education, performing arts, dance and sports science, resort health and wellness programmes, and fitness. This opportunity was funded by a generous award through ICURe (Innovation to Commercialisation of University Research), under the auspices of the Directorate of Research and Enterprise (R&E) at Queen's University, Belfast, in collaboration with the universities of Bath, Bristol, Exeter, Southampton, and Surrey.

The researcher travelled for meetings to several cities throughout Italy, the United States, England, Scotland, Germany, Sweden, and Hong Kong. The interviewees who participated in one-to-one meetings with the researcher included (in order of interview):

- Dr Luigi Cucchi, Giornalista e Direttore, Il Giornale, Milan, Italy

- Gian Luca Schiavoni, Ballet Dancer and Choreographer, Teatro alla Scala; and Chiara Schiavoni, Ballet Dancer, Teatro alla Scala, Milan, Italy

- Serap Mesutogeu, Guest Relations, Four Seasons Hotels and Resorts, Milan, Italy

- Dr Roberto Pozzoni, Specialista Ortopedia e Traumatologia, Milan, Italy

- Elena Cervellati, Associate Professor, Arts Department, University of Bologna, Italy

- Rocco Di Michele, Associate Professor, Department of Biomedical and Neuromotor Sciences, University of Bologna, Italy

- Felice Limosani, Multidisciplinary Artist, and Doris Anna Kovacs, Libero Professionista, Florence, Italy

- Jamie Harris, Director/Agent, Clear Talent Group, New York, New York, United States

- Carol Espel, Fitness and Program Director, Pritikin Longevity Center and Spa, New York, New York, United States

- Dr Kimberly Chandler Vaccaro, Associate Professor of Dance, Rider University, Ewing, New Jersey, United States

- Emily Bakemeier, Deputy Provost Yale University, New Haven, Connecticut, United States

- James Bundy, Dean of the Yale School of Drama and Artistic Director of Yale Repertory Theatre, New Haven, Connecticut, United States

- Todd Lanman, MD, Spinal Neurosurgeon, Los Angeles, California, United States

- Jonas Wright, Dean and Chief Academic Officer of the San Francisco Conservatory of Music, California, United States

- Tak Friedman and Terry Berg, Wellness Team, Rosewood Resort, Hong Kong, China

- William Baugh, The Tina Turner Musical, Hamburg, Germany

- Dr Susan Kozel, Professor of Philosophy, Dance and Media Technologies, Malmo University, Sweden

- Margaret Morris Movement, West Sussex, United Kingdom

- Catherine Cassidy, Director, and Lisa Sinclair, Dance Health Manager, The Scottish Ballet, Glasgow, Scotland, United Kingdom

- Chrissy Delapperall, Manager Virgin Active, Chelmsford, United Kingdom

- Dr Emma Redding, Head of Dance Science, Trinity Laban Conservatoire of Music and Dance, London, United Kingdom

- Dr Marcus Dunn, Research Fellow, Centre of Sports Engineering Research, Sheffield Hallam University, Sheffield, United Kingdom

# Films & Documentaries

### *An Interview with Esther Fairfax*

### *Part 1 and Part 2*

Jacobs, J. R. & Buckley, A. (2017). *An Interview with Esther Fairfax* (video-recorded documentary). (Hungerford, Berkshire). Available at: Part 1 - https://youtu.be/JvGn6DGrJiY and Part 2 - https://www.dropbox.com/s/c7veuqt9e4axgo2/Esther%20Interview%20Part%202.mp4?dl=0

In Fairfax's 2010 book, *My Improper Mother and Me*, there is a gap in Lotte Berk's history that comes at a pivotal time in the inception of her programme. Although the literature references a car accident as being the catalyst for the development of her programme for the purpose of rehabilitating her injuries, in reality, Berk was recovering from the breakup of an intense love relationship as well as a morphine addiction. This point and other details of Berk's backstory were clarified during the researcher's video-recorded interview with Esther Fairfax, Lotte Berk's daughter.

### *Jill Rose Jacobs Dance Study*

---. (2018). *Jill Rose Jacobs Dance Study* (video-recorded documentary). (Belfast: Queen's University, Movement Innovation Lab). Available at: https://youtu.be/HlBkEQ6MCNY

This study, *A comparison of Barre and Zumba/Dance Fit on standing leg stability and on the physiological and psychological impact of musical accompaniment on overall movement quality*, was conducted in the Movement Innovation Lab at the Physical Education Centre at Queen's University, Belfast. Using 3D Qualisy motion capture and force platform systems, participants performed a one-legged dynamic balance test to two sound conditions: with musical accompaniment, and using verbal-only cues (without music). A panel of expert evaluators, Sarita Allen, Alvin Ailey Dance Theatre; Elisabeth Halfpapp and Fred DeVito, creators/owners of CoreBarreFit; Dr Alan Cummins, Project Lead Developer at ARLive Systems; Kedzie Penfield, Analytic Psychotherapist and Counsellor; and Peggy Hackney, EMOVE Institute, were asked to score individual participants' performances.

### *The High Barre: A PhD Journey with Jill Rose Jacobs*

Jacobs, J. R.; Moloney, D.; & Murphy, P. *The High Barre: A PhD Journey with Jill Rose Jacobs*. (Belfast: Queen's University and Crescent Arts Centre). Available at https://youtu.be/Jiu_o68IGsE

Does Barre methodology's fitness/arts approach present a uniquely modernised, dance-based foundation that can benefit learners in higher education performing arts and in various dance-movement programmes in other fields? This film follows the researcher's doctoral journey and synthesizes her experience and investigations.

# Table of Contents

**Table of Figures**

# Acknowledgements

Deepest gratitude and appreciation to my Queen's University, Belfast, advisors Dr Franziska Schroeder, Reader, School of Arts, English and Languages, and Dr Matthew Rodger, Senior Lecturer, School of Psychology, and to doctoral panellist Dr David Grant, Senior Lecturer in the School of Creative Arts, and Dr Emma Redding, Head of Dance Science at Trinity Laban Conservatoire of Music and Dance. Thank you, Dr Cahal McLaughlin, Chair of Film Studies, Queen's University, Belfast, for your mentorship.

Thank you to the community of Queen's University, Belfast, and to my Barre family at Crescent Arts Centre and Queen's University Physical Education Centre. My sincere gratitude to the participants in the pilot studies: Case Study 1 and Case Study 2 and to expert evaluators Sarita Allen, Alvin Ailey Dance Theatre; Elisabeth Halfpapp and Fred DeVito, creators/owners of CoreBarreFit; Dr Alan Cummins, Project Lead Developer at ARLive Systems; Kedzie Penfield, Analytic Psychotherapist and Counsellor; and Peggy Hackney, EMOVE Institute, for your contributions, and to Queen's University Tech Support Services for staffing the equipment used in the studies.

Deepest appreciation to ICURe and the universities of Bath, Bristol, Exeter, Southampton, Surrey, and Queen's University, Belfast, and to the ICURe team: Don Spalinger, Director of Corporate Relations, University of Southampton; Thea Glasspool, ICURe Programme Officer; Alan Scrase, Access to Mentoring and Finance Lead; Lisa McMullan, Director & Consultancy at The Women's Organisation & Enterprise Evolution; Simon Brown, CEO at P2T Consulting Ltd.; and Rob Yates, Director at Yaltec Ltd. Tremendous thanks to The High Barre team: Jason Wiggins, SetSquared ICURe Programme Manager at the University of Southampton; Hilmar Noble, CEO at Noble Advisory Partners; and Claudio Castiglioni, Co-founder and President, Beauty Thinkers. Thank you Dean James Bundy, Yale School of Drama and Artistic Director of the Yale Repertory Theatre; Dean Jonas Wright, Chief Academic Officer of the San Francisco Conservatory of Music; Emily Bakemeier, Deputy Provost Yale University; Dr Marcus Dunn, Research Fellow, Centre of Sports Engineering Research, Sheffield Hallam University; Dr Susan Kozel, Professor of Philosophy, Dance and Media Technologies, Malmo University; Dr Todd Lanman, Spinal Neurosurgery; Dr Roberto Pozzoni, Specialista Ortopedia e Traumatologia; Margaret Morris Movement; Elena Cervellati, Professor of the Arts, University of Bologna;

Rocco Di Michele, Associate Professor, Department of Biomedical and Neuromotor Sciences, University of Bologna; Dr Kimberly Chandler Vaccaro, Associate Professor of Dance, Rider University; Jamie Harris, Director/Agent, Clear Talent Group; Carol Espel, Fitness and Program Director, Pritikin Longevity Center and Spa; Gianluca Schiavoni, Ballet Dancer and Choreographer, Teatro alla Scala; Chiara Shiavoni, Ballerina, Teatro alla Scala; Felice Limosani, Multidisciplinary Artist; Doris Anna Kovacs, Libero Professionista, Florence Yes Please; Serap Mesutogeu, Guest Relations, Four Seasons Hotels and Resorts; Dr Luigi Cucchi, Giornalista, Direttore Il Giornale; William Baugh, *The Tina Turner Musical*, Hamburg; Catherine Cassidy, Director, and Lisa Sinclair, Dance Health Manager, The Scottish Ballet, Glasgow; Chrissy Delapperall, Manager Virgin Active; and the wellness team at Rosewood Resort for your contributions. Deep reverence to Shona Morris, Lead Movement Tutor, Royal Academy of Dramatic Arts, for your inspiration.

Thank you, Paula Johnston and Denise Toner, School of Arts, English, and Languages, Queen's University, Belfast, for your production assistance; and to The High Barre team: Bernadette Kenna, owner of Love Lotte; Anita O'Connor, Mother and Solicitor; Cindy Léonet, Engineer, Production Management; Lynsey Caroline, Image Consultant with Colour Me Beautiful; Dr Ellen Pollheimer, MD; and Aimee Buckley, Owner of New Generation Film. Thank you ROC Nation for the use of 'Love on the Brain'; to the Grand Central Hotel for the use of your location; Neil Ritchie, Hanna IP; and Donal Moloney, Director, Producer, Editor, and Assistant Editor, Donal Moloney Photography, and Patricia Murphy, Assistant, Donal Moloney Photography, for producing and recording of 'The High Barre: A PhD journey with Jill Rose Jacobs'.

For information about the history of Barre and Lotte Berk, I'd like to thank Jo Fairfax, Esther Fairfax, Lydia Bach, Anne Cheshire, and Lady Diana Waterloo.

My deepest gratitude to my husband, Declan Mooney; dear friends Claudio Castiglioni and Dina Rezvanipour; and to my editor, Pam Day.

# Introduction

The traditional use of the word barre may bring to mind ballerinas in ballet class. However, over recent years the term has become associated with the programme known as Barre, a popular fitness regimen in the United States and United Kingdom (Saedi, 2015; London, 2015; MacVean, 2015; Travers, 2019; Thomason, 2021). And while Barre is currently understood as a fitness programme, this thesis will propose that Barre also may be understood as an arts-based programme, as it was originally intended by its founder, Lotte Berk, and highly suitable for the performing arts in higher education.

Barre was innovated by Lotte Berk in 1959 as a dance-based programme that offered women physical and psychological benefits, such as improvements in muscle strength, tone, posture, mood, and confidence (Berk and Prince, 1978). Berk considered her programme to be a performance art, underpinned by contemporary ballet, which had been a passion for her. Berk's emphasis, therefore, was on the performing arts aspect of her creation rather than on the fitness focus that Barre is known for today. To put the development and evolution of Barre into context, it is important to examine Lotte Berk's personal history and how it informed the innovation of her programme.

## What is the Motivation for and Aim of this Thesis?

In the researcher's performing arts classroom at New York University (NYU), where the researcher taught dance combined with Barre elements for seventeen years, learners of different backgrounds and disciplines, including drama, dance, opera, musical theatre, musicians, and others, were combined in dance classes in which participation was required to fulfil various performing arts degrees. Combining learners from different disciplines is common in the university performing arts setting, in contrast to performing arts academies, where students are divided by age and level of proficiency and trained according to traditional methods of dance.

In addition to the researcher's background in higher education, she instructed Barre programmes for a leading fitness franchise in New York City, where it was common to have forty-five participants of varied demographics, ranging from ages 18 to 70, in the same class. In the fitness studio environment, the researcher noted that with time and practise, the participants experienced physiological and psychological improvements manifested by changes in muscle strength; body shape; posture; movement quality and control; confidence, both in-class and outside the studio; and in mood, as evidenced by participants' physical and facial expressions. Moreover, the researcher noted that students in both the fitness and university classroom settings performed better when movements were choreographed and paired to musical accompaniment.

The students in the researcher's courses at NYU, regardless of their prior dance experience, performing arts discipline, or physical condition, demonstrated improvements in dance technique, musicality, expressivity, and artistry over the course of their four-year programme as a result of the integrated teaching modality of dance/Barre. In the researcher's experience, also having instructed in dance academies that use traditional methods, her university students' improvements were greater and developed within a shorter timeframe when aspects of Barre methodology were combined with traditional methods of dance training. These observations motivated the researcher to enter doctoral study to investigate dance/Barre training methodologies to maximize positive aspects of the learner's experience in university dance education programmes.

**What are the Research Questions?**

Based on the researcher's background and motivation to improve dance education in university performing arts curricula, this thesis queries the following:

- What is Barre methodology, its origins, and how was it developed?
- How is Barre currently being practised and does the methodology have potential applications beyond fitness and dance?
- How does Barre's relationship to both fitness and the performing arts potentially benefit learners in dance education performing arts programmes?
- How can Barre's benefits, such as those observed by the researcher and claimed by Barre enthusiasts in the media, be scientifically studied?
- Do the thesis research results support the integration of Barre methodology into performing arts curricula in higher education?

As this research is novel to academic study on the subject of Barre, the investigations aim to answer these questions through review of the existing literature, media sources, ethnographic interviews, qualitative and quantitative study, and in video-recorded documentaries used to support the information in this thesis.

**How does the thesis answer the research questions?**

*What is Barre Methodology, its Origins, and How was it Developed?*

This thesis is structured to establish the historic and biographic origins of Barre, then build on this information to explore the methodology and its evolution. This approach serves as preparation for the following investigations by recording the underpinnings and principles of Barre methodology and how practitioners benefit from its practises. This strategy relied on several methods for data collection and a broad-stroke approach for understanding the potential applications for Barre methodology and its potential placement in dance education for the performing arts.

Early in doctoral research, the literature and media sources revealed conflicting reports about Berk and the motivation for her original programme and propagated a backstory for Berk and her exercise method that was based on misinformation. The researcher had received Barre teacher training at a leading fitness franchise in New York City which taught that Barre was developed by Lotte Berk as a self-rehabilitation programme to recover from severe spinal injuries suffered in a car accident that left her confined to a wheelchair. At the time of entering the doctoral programme at Queen's University, Belfast, the researcher believed this claim to be true.

The process of piecing together information from the literature led the researcher to interview Esther Fairfax, Lotte Berk's daughter, and create the video-documentary *An Interview with Esther Fairfax*. During the course of this interview, Fairfax revealed that a morphine addiction developed during a failed relationship was actually the catalyst for Berk to create her programme as a means for physical, psychological, and financial recovery. Drawing on her passions for music and dance, Berk devised her original programme, which she called Rehabilitative Exercise. According to Fairfax:

> Mother had lost the love of her life and at the same time decided that she would get herself off drugs completely… She was addicted to morphine as well as sleeping pills . . . For months I saw little of my mother as she battled on her own. She shut herself in her flat, drowning herself with loud music, Beethoven and Bach accompanied our telephone conversations. (Fairfax, 2010, pp. 71-72)
>
> . . . And when that [her relationship] broke up, well, Lotte didn't work during the time with Cynthia [her lover]. She felt like she was retiring anyways so that

happened then. Lotte was addicted but had no source – she could not get drugs. (*An Interview with Esther Fairfax*, 2017)

The video-documentary served as an effort to fill in the gaps and correct the historical information about Berk that exists in the current literature and media sources. However, other interviews that the researcher conducted with close associates of Berk's, including Lydia Bach, Berk's original licensee of thirty-five years, also revealed that Fairfax and Berk's relationship had been estranged for nearly thirty years, shedding doubt on the reliability of Fairfax's knowledge of Berk's programme, especially considering that Fairfax's background and education did not include training in dance, music, or the performing arts, as did her mother's.

Chapter 1 provides biographical information about Berk and her programme and follows the methodology's evolution through to its many present-day iterations in both the United States and the United Kingdom.

### *How is Barre currently being practised and does the methodology have potential applications beyond fitness and dance?*

The first section of Chapter 2 examines current teacher training manuals for Barre, classical ballet, and theatre arts, and reviews the research in the fields of dance and sports science.

The dance and sports research studies highlight a lack of fitness conditioning in traditional dance training and recommend supplementary fitness conditioning to augment the traditional methods. The studies are specific in their assessment of where the current dance training falls short and the types of conditioning that have been found beneficial. These details are explored in Chapter 2, as well as the ways that Barre can be tailored to match various fitness objectives.

The second section of Chapter 2 presents a global ethnographic investigation, conducted under the auspices of ICURe (Innovation to Commercialism of University Research), in which the researcher travelled to numerous cities throughout Italy, the United States, the United Kingdom, Sweden, Scotland, Germany, and Hong Kong to meet with experts and leaders in the fields of medicine, media, education, the performing arts, resort wellbeing programmes, and fitness. The aim of this investigation was to gain knowledge and insight from experts to assess how Barre methodology could be tailored for applications beyond its current placement in fitness as well as identify concerns that Barre could be used to address.

The interviews and process of synthesizing the data contributed to clarifying Barre methodology's relationship to fitness and the arts, which motivated the discussion that follows in Chapter 3.

### How does Barre's relationship to both fitness and the performing arts benefit learners in dance education in the performing arts?

Chapter 3 examines Barre's relationship to fitness and dance to understand the methodology's potential for application in university performing arts curricula. An examination of the literature provides historical perspectives, including the original training methods of the Danish Bournonville style of classical ballet and the conditioning regimen of renowned nineteenth-century ballerina Marie Taglioni to the current-day teaching practices of George Balanchine, 'the father of the Neoclassical style in American ballet'.

In higher education, dance education programmes have shared a history with physical education from the creation of the first dance programme in 1926 at the University of Wisconsin, Madison, by Margaret D'Houbler, whose background was in biology and sports science. D'Houbler's dance education programme was, and remains, resident in the university's department of physical education.

### How can Barre's benefits, such as those observed by the researcher and claimed by Barre enthusiasts in the media, be scientifically studied?

Chapters 1 through 3 established an understanding of Barre's history and methodology and outlined its potential that could then be expanded into case studies. In Chapter 4, Case Study 1: 'Self-reported physiological and psychological effects of Barre compared with Zumba/Dance Fit' used a questionnaire designed and distributed to learners in Barre, Zumba, and Dance Fit programmes to collect data about their dance-fitness experience. The Physical Education Centre (PEC) at Queen's University, Belfast, and the Crescent Arts Centre (CAC), located on campus, provided volunteers for the study.

In Chapter 5, Case Study 2: 'A comparison of Barre and Zumba/Dance Fit on standing leg stability and the physiological and psychological impact of musical accompaniment on overall movement quality' further expands on Case Study 1. The participants in the study visited the Movement Innovation Lab (MIL) and performed a choreographed Barre sequence that was recorded using 3D motion capture and force platform equipment. To analyse the data, three experts in the fields of dance and sports science, two Laban Movement Analysts, and a systems specialist evaluated the participants' individual recordings and scored their performances based on a demonstration of technical skills. A video-recording of a participant in the MIL performing the choreographed Barre sequence and one-legged dynamic balance test has been attached to this thesis.

**What does the thesis recommend for the future?**

***Do the thesis research results support the integration of Barre methodology into performing arts curricula in higher education?***

This thesis supports the potential for Barre methodology to be used in dance education for the performing arts in higher education and beyond. Barre's origin, its evolution and relationship to sports/fitness conditioning and the performing arts/dance, its benefits to learners, and its potential to be tailored to supplement traditional dance training are all highlighted in the research and form the basis for recommending Barre's implementation into university dance education curricula.

In the original Appendices section of this thesis, the researcher provided two original manuals to facilitate the integration of Barre methodology into the university performing arts classroom. *The High Barre: Barre for the performing arts in higher education* outlines the structure and content for tailoring Barre practises for dance, and *The Jacobs Method of Notation* features a user-friendly system for choreographing Barre practises that may be used in various performing arts disciplines. A short film, *The High Barre*, is attached to this thesis and documents the researcher's journey through the process of doctoral study. Manuals available at www.jillrosejacobs.com.

# Chapter 1. Barre of the Past: What is Barre and How Has it Evolved? A Brief History of Lotte Berk

Born Lieselotte "Lotte" Heymansohn (13 January 1913 – 4 November 2003), Berk grew up in a well-to-do home in Cologne, Germany. Her father was a successful tailor and business owner, and her mother's family owned a horse and carriage delivery service that carried goods throughout her hometown. In *My Improper Mother and Me*, a book written in 2010 by Berk's daughter, Esther Fairfax, Berk presents her recollection of a loving family life: 'Our apartment was above father's shop. He came up and had lunch with us every day, saying he couldn't go the whole day without seeing his lovely family' (Fairfax, 2010, p. 4). Berk's father designed and made the clothes for Berk and her sister and took them for rides in his luxurious Mercedes-Benz 770K. However, when Berk was 8 years old, her mother died of a stroke during their family's lunchtime gathering, an event that sent her father into a deep mourning that greatly impacted their home life.

From an early age, Berk's father wanted her to become a concert pianist; however, Berk found her passion in dance. In Fairfax's 2010 book, Berk is recorded stating: 'My body ached to dance. After my final exam I broke the news to father. He was bitterly disappointed. Of course, he still let me go to the academy' (Fairfax, 2010, pp. 4, 7). This 'academy' that Berk purportedly attended was the prestigious Mary Wigman Academy of Dance (Fairfax, 2010). Further research revealed, however, that the claims regarding Berk's attendance at the renowned school, which was located in Dresden, were exaggerated. In Berk's hometown of Cologne, she studied with a female Russian teacher who had attended the Mary Wigman Academy of Dance (Fairfax, J., 2021).

On her first visit to the dance school, a 'gawky young man', Ernest Berk, opened the door for her. Ernest, also a dancer, would become her husband in 1933, when she was 20 years old (Fairfax, 2010, pp. 4, 7). Soon after their marriage, they were forced to escape Nazi-occupied Germany and relocate to London, a move made possible by Ernest's British passport. Berk was recorded telling the following story in 1984, as noted in Fairfax's book:

> By 1934 I was an established dancer with a star-studded career ahead of me. In July 1934, I gave birth to my daughter, Esther, and three weeks later I was a solo dancer in the Salzburg Festival. I was tasting fame and loving it. Soon the air of persecution was seeping into our daily lives. Jews were forbidden to sit in the cafes. 'Jew' became a dirty word. Fear was like a silent fog that chilled the air.

Ernest and I were due to give a recital. About two hours before the performance we had a call. It was the Gestapo. They warned me that if I went on stage they would arrest me. Ernest could perform, as he was not Jewish. Leaflets were distributed that said, 'If you are a good Nazi you will not attend this performance.' I felt rage tear through my body. No one tells me what I can or cannot do. My stubborn streak ruled me. I had a British passport, thanks to Ernest, and they couldn't touch me. My friends tried to talk sense to me . . . The theatre was quite full but hushed. SS men stood in strategic positions along the side of the auditorium. With my heart thumping I stood hidden backstage in the wings. The director announced that I would not be performing and Ernest would dance as though I was. He gestured for me to come forward. I walked onto the stage and someone appeared and presented me with a large bouquet of flowers. I retreated clutching my flowers, giving a bow back into the wings as Ernest danced. You could almost see me with him as he gestured to where I would have been had I been dancing. At the end the audience broke into thunderous applause and cried out, 'Dance Lotte, dance!' I felt triumphant and came forward. More flowers were thrown at my feet. As the applause died down, I shouted out to them, 'Thank you for not being Nazis!' Immediately the waiting SS rushed onto the stage screaming, 'Out, out!' (Fairfax, 2010, pp. 8, 9)

In London, Berk modeled at Chelsea Art School, and, on occasion, she danced for Madame Rambert. Berk later toured with the Entertainments National Service Association (ENSA) but was disheartened that her preferred style of contemporary dance was not appreciated in the English cultural milieu of the day (Fairfax, 2010). Berk would also learn that her father had been captured by the Nazis in 1941, and died in Auschwitz in 1943. In London, Berk's already eccentric, and often scandalous, behavior extended into her lifestyle, which was filled with a continuous stream of lovers (Kirsch, 2004; Fairfax, 2010; Friedman, 2018).

Through an historic lens, it is also relevant to consider how these events may have affected Berk's daughter, who was 4 years old at the time of their arrival in London. In Fairfax's book, she portrays her home life as filled with unimaginable abuse. Fairfax speaks of Berk's lifestyle; her lovers, who at times lived in the house with the family; and being sent to boarding school, where Fairfax was physically abused, to accommodate her mother's time with lovers (Fairfax, 2010, pp. 21-24).

This abusive upbringing affected Fairfax's development and confidence, and at the age of 15, Fairfax left school altogether. A month after Fairfax's 18th birthday, she married a writer, John Fairfax. When they wed, Fairfax was already six months pregnant with his child (Fairfax, 2010, p. 44). As Berk's success grew in London, however, Fairfax and her family were living in poverty. 'We ended up living hand to mouth in cottages which had been condemned with no running water or a lavatory' (Yaffe, 2017).

In Fairfax's 2010 book, there is a gap in Lotte Berk's history that comes at a pivotal time in the inception of her programme. Although the literature references a car accident as being the catalyst for the development of her programme for the purpose of rehabilitating her injuries (Feeney, 2017; Saxon, 2003; Crowther, 2017; Rosenstein and Arkin, 2014), in reality, Berk was recovering from the breakup of an intense love relationship as well as a morphine addiction. Fairfax asserts: 'Mother had lost the love of her life and at the same time decided that she would get herself off drugs completely… She was addicted to morphine as well as sleeping pills' (Fairfax, 2010, pp. 71-72).

In the 1978 book, *The Lotte Berk Method of Exercise*, that Berk co-authored with her friend Jean Prince, Berk's reticence about this difficult phase of her life appears as a veiled reference, the details of which Berk never wanted to disclose:

> Eventually Lotte's need for love overtook her need for dancing . . . But this, her greatest love, became her greatest tragedy. The end was so sad that Lotte will never talk about it. Anything else she will happily disclose, but this chapter of her life must remain untold. (Berk & Prince, 1978)

This point was clarified during the researcher's video-recorded interview with Fairfax, during which she explained:

> Well, you know that Cynthia [Berk's lover] was a drug addict and Lotte became one, as well. Cynthia was an absolutely lovely person. When you think drug addict, you always think of a person that is down and out. But Cynthia was a very beautiful person with a very beautiful soul. Tragic circumstances led to her being a drug addict. She actually tried to be a doctor but before she quite finished being qualified, she turned to drugs . . . Because they were drug addicts, they spent a lot of time being at home and chatting, meeting, injecting. And when that broke up, well, Lotte didn't work during the time with Cynthia. She felt like she was retiring anyways so that happened then. Lotte was addicted but had no source – she could not get drugs. Cynthia knew how to get drugs . . . Lotte had to go cold turkey. And I think if you've been addicted to anything, to go cold turkey like that takes huge strength. She may have been a difficult person, but what strength that woman had. (*An Interview with Esther Fairfax*, 2017)

It was during the time Berk was detoxing that she began devising the programme that would evolve into Barre. Berk drew on her passions for dance and music for inspiration. 'For months I saw little of my mother as she battled on her own. She shut herself in her flat, drowning herself with loud music, Beethoven and Bach accompanied our telephone conversations' (Fairfax, 2010, p. 72). The literature gives few details about this period and is silent on specific dates.

Many of the media sources, as well as Fairfax's 2010 book, claim that Berk was encouraged at this time, the late 1950s, by her friend Ann Mankowitz to create an exercise program that was different from the military-type workouts that were popular during this period (Fairfax, 2010, pp. 72-73). Ann and her husband, Wolf, who was a writer and film producer, regularly socialised with celebrities and promised to support Berk by attending her classes and introducing her to their influential friends. Fairfax writes: 'Pretty young starlets, writers, actors known for their serious work and celebrities known for very little, models and journalists all had a place on the green carpet in the basement of her [Berk's] infamous studio . . .' (Fairfax, 2010, p.73).

**Berk's Innovation: Rehabilitative Exercise**

Berk's program was launched from a basement studio on Manchester Street in 1959 (Fairfax, 2010, pp. 80-81). Fairfax's description of the premises best illustrates the dichotomy between the location and the clients who would become her loyal followers:

> . . . hers [Berk's] had been a milliner's factory when she took it over . . . she arranged for the barres to be installed, chose fitted carpet, had a tiny loo installed in a corner of the passage that led from the basement entrance. No matter that the only window, and only chance for students to get some fresh air, was very small, facing a brick wall . . . the air that came down through this window was mainly fumes from the constant passing flow of traffic in the street above. (Fairfax, 2010, pp. 80-81)

Berk's celebrity devotees are documented in the literature as including Joan Collins, Britt Ekland, Siân Phillips, Edna O'Brien, Yasmin Le Bon, Zoë Wanamaker, Maureen Lipman, Prue Leith, Shirley Conran, Barbara Ferris, Lee Remick, Carol Linley, Yolande Donlan, Beverly Sassoon, and Barbra Streisand (Berk & Prince, 1978; Jardine, 2010; Welsh, 2003; Fairfax, 2010; Bach, 2020).

In Berk and Prince's 1978 book, Prince speaks of her first experience in Berk's class, offering one of the earliest documented testimonials to be found:

After a two-hour journey from the coast, I approach her studio in London with nervousness. I had heard so much about Lotte's method of exercise, and being extremely unfit I wondered if I could survive. But the promise of a slimmer figure, renewed vigour and vitality together with a feeling of being 'so alive' rang in my ears. So what if it was hard work? The fulfilment of Lotte's promise must surely make it all worthwhile . . . As we warm-up (I feel like I am over-heating!), Lotte chats gaily with an effervescence that is contagious . . . the class moves to the barre. Like a ballet rehearsal we stand in a line along the wall . . . 'Squat on your feet, heels clicked together, knees open wide. Come up an inch. Hold. Up an inch more. Hold. Down and inch. Hold. She [Lotte] always asks questions in the middle of an exercise . . . Only a few minutes pass and I'm already feeling muscles that I didn't know I had. The exercises continue at a fast pace . . . The class ends – the forty-five minutes are up (it seemed like a lifetime to me) and my legs feel like jelly.

Berk and Prince's 1978 book also suggests choosing 'some gay lively music that makes you feel good, and do all the exercises in rhythm with the music—just let your body flow and move as if you were dancing'.

Other than this very early testimony, the existing sources focus on and speak about Berk's eccentric lifestyle and her outrageous in-class commentary. Provocatively named exercises— including 'Swingers', 'The Peeing Dog', 'The Prostitute', and 'The French Lavatory'—caused hilarity that became a hallmark of Berk's teaching style (Jardine, 2010; Welch, 2003; Fairfax, 2010; Halfpapp, 2019; Cheshire, 2019). Fairfax and others cite examples of the sexual banter so characteristic of Berk's approach:

Frequently when working a position that was particularly hard to hold, mother would hone in on the first person that caught her eye. 'No, no, hold it. Tell me, did you have sex last night? You're looking a little tired. No, no, keep holding . . .'. (Fairfax, 2010, pp. 81-82)

Lotte definitely followed a methodology with some 'winging it'. Some exercises had variations, but they all came with humour or sexual innuendo that made everyone laugh. 'Stretch your arms into the air . . . now compare the size of your diamonds'. (Cheshire, 2019)

I was a young woman, newlywed at the time. When I would go home and tell my husband what we did in class and what Lotte had said . . . he would reply, 'Impossible! I don't believe you!' (Waterloo, 2019)

While Berk fueled the sensationalized reports that contributed to the rise of her success and notoriety, the actual *substance* and *methodology* of Berk's original innovation was largely overlooked. Moreover, Berk never produced a teacher training manual (Bach, 2020; Cheshire,

2019; Halfpapp, 2019; Kenna, 2019). In an effort to ascertain Berk's original methodology, the researcher sought clarification by interviewing participants of Berk's classes and/or those who were certified by her.

## Ethnographic Interviews

### *Esther Fairfax and Lotte Berk*

In an effort to establish an historical timeline and fill the gaps through testimony for the development of Barre, the researcher conducted a series of ethnographic interviews with close associates and acolytes of Lotte Berk. The interviewees include former student Lady Diana Waterloo; Berk's teacher trainee, Anne Cheshire; Berk's thirty-five-year licensee, Lydia Bach; Bach's employee of twenty-two years, Elisabeth Halfpapp; Berk's daughter, Esther Fairfax; and Fairfax's former assistant, Bernadette Kenna.

The interviews were conducted by the researcher in one-to-one meetings and in telephone conversations that have been transcribed for use in this thesis. Moreover, the closed-captioned video-documentary of the interview with Fairfax has also been submitted to substantiate the claims made in this thesis. In addition to the interviewees' conversations and the classes the researcher took with them, the interviewees also contributed manuals, photographs, and written communications that provided source materials for this thesis (Fairfax, Kenna, & Whee, 2016; Bach, 1973; DeVito & Halfpapp, 2013, 2015). The information and data gathered have been critically analyzed and cross-referenced in order to ferret out the veracity of Lotte Berk's story as presented in often-conflicting reports in the literature and other written sources.

Fairfax is often quoted as the definitive source in the literature for information about her mother and Berk's innovation. However, during the interview process, it came to light that Fairfax and Berk had been estranged from about 1969 until shortly before Berk was institutionalized for dementia, around 1997-98 (Fairfax, 2010, p. 292). Of the interviewees—Waterloo, Halfpapp, Cheshire, and Lydia Bach, Berk's licensee of thirty-five years—not one of them had actually met with or spoken to Fairfax (Bach, 2018; Cheshire, 2019; Halfpapp, 2019; Waterloo, 2019).

It becomes evident that by the time Bach began her training with Berk in 1969, Fairfax was not part of Berk's life (Bach, 2018). In Bach's interview, she states that during the period of her training with Berk, Fairfax never once appeared at the studio. Fairfax explains her absence

6

during this period: '…eventually, in 1970, I could see no way to restore our friendship. I decided to give up my studio and to no longer run classes… I hoped that she [Berk] would see me as her daughter, as her only child, and we would be the greatest of friends as before' (Fairfax, 2010, p. 102). Also in 1970, Berk and Bach entered into a licensing agreement that would enable Bach to open The Lotte Berk Method studio in New York City in 1971. Shortly thereafter, Fairfax attempted suicide, as described in her book:

> Once I stopped the exercises, the downward spiral accelerated rapidly . . . After the [Berk's] boyfriend left, mother went to bed. I went to the sitting room where my bed was. I sat down, staring into space, when my eyes focused on the bottle of whisky mother always kept for her lover. With little thought I unscrewed the top of the bottle and took a mouthful of the neat whiskey. It burnt as it went down. At last, I could see a way out of my black pit. In a little while it would be over. I tried to crunch up sleeping pills in my teeth but they tasted so bitter. I tried swallowing as many as I could into one go, washing them down with the whiskey, again and again, one horrible mouthful after another. I stopped suddenly, remembering something mother once said. Anyone committing suicide should always leave a note to help the people left behind to understand. I fumbled as I wrote my note, my hands shaking. Already the whisky and pills were taking effect. Once the note was done, I continued with the whisky and pills. I can't remember what I wrote. I slipped into oblivion. (Fairfax, 2010, pp. 111, 113)

The ordeal would later initiate changes in Fairfax as a result of therapy with a psychiatrist (Fairfax, 2010, p. 127), a process that would give her the confidence and motivation to make changes to her mother's programme, thus creating a method of her own. When Fairfax resumed teaching after this seven-year hiatus and without the aid of a written manual, she would have taught from memory, based on the limited training she had had with her mother in London once a week in 1962-63 (Fairfax, 2010, p. 84). It is notable that Berk never produced a written teacher's manual that Fairfax could have used as a guideline (Bach, 2018; Fairfax, 2010; Kenna, 2020; Halfpapp, 2018; Cheshire, 2019).

In 1978, Fairfax published a book, *Help Yourself to Health: Exercises That Really Work for Men and Women*, that was comprised of her mother's exercises without Berk's permission, a decision that infuriated Berk. Fairfax's method was a departure from her mother's contemporary ballet-based program. Moreover, the sexual innuendo and risqué exercise names found in Berk's programme were replaced in Fairfax's with generic exercise descriptions (Fairfax, 1978).

Fairfax's 1978 book pre-empted one that Berk had been working on with Jean Prince, *The Lotte Berk Method of Exercise*, that was slated to be released that same year. Following

Fairfax's book release, Berk penned an angry note to Fairfax that exclaimed above her signature, 'The End of Mother and Daughter!' (Fairfax, 2010, p. 134) This estrangement between mother and daughter goes a long way to explaining the differences between how Berk's programme evolved in the United States through Bach versus the form it took in the United Kingdom through Fairfax.

These notable differences came to light after the researcher attended classes with Fairfax (2017- 2019), Halfpapp (2018, 2019, 2021), Kenna (2017-2021), and Cheshire (2019), in which the researcher observed divergences from Fairfax's technique in their class structure and content, terminology, and methodology. Cheshire's and Halfpapp's classes incorporated elements of dance theory and terminology, a tell-tale sign of Berk's training. This assertion can be stated with confidence because while Halfpapp was an accomplished ballet dancer, Cheshire had no exposure to dance (either before training with Berk, or after), so the similarity between the two women's classes is clear evidence of Berk's programme having provided the original source material for both.

Conversely, the use of dance theory and terminology are entirely absent in Fairfax's programme, as noted by the researcher's observations as well as Halfpapp's and Cheshire's commentaries after their review of Fairfax's 2016 manual (Cheshire, 2019; Halfpapp, 2019). Cues and ballet-based verbal instructions that Halfpapp and Cheshire integrate are absent from Fairfax's programme. These notable differences will be further examined in Chapters 2 and 3.

### *Lydia Bach and Lotte Berk*

Certain commonalities existed between Lydia Bach and Esther Fairfax: They were close in age, both had abusive mothers, and had mother/daughter relationships that were fraught (Bach, 2019-2020; Fairfax, 2010). While the two young women experienced similar relational hardship with their mothers, the manner in which they reacted to the abuse diverged dramatically. Whereas Fairfax constantly sought her mother's approval and exhibited emotional dependency, Bach became wildly independent and eccentric. In this way, Bach shared more in common with Berk than Berk shared with her own daughter.

Before arriving in London, Bach had been trekking from Malaysia to Lebanon (Bach, 2018). Once in London, her connection with Berk began around 1969, when Bach's friend Britt Ekland invited Bach to Berk's exercise class, which was considered 'all the rage' at the time:

The sign on the door read: Rehabilitative Exercise. The studio was no more than three-hundred square feet, and it had worn-out carpet and was quite dingy . . . There were people lying on top of other people. You couldn't tell right away who people were and that everyone was more or less rich or famous. And they didn't tell their other friends about the studio or Lotte. It was sort of a private club. (Bach, 2018)

Bach was inspired by Berk's exercises, but also admired her character. 'She stood onstage and spoke out against the Nazis in front of an audience' (Bach, 2020). When Bach began training with Berk in her 'L-shaped' studio, Bach positioned herself in a way that Berk couldn't see her modifying the exercises. Another student in the class noticed Bach's modifications and quipped, 'You should do what you're doing and make some money' (Bach, 2018). It was comments from fellow students and a *New York Times* article about fashion designer Halston licensing his name that served as a catalyst for Bach to approach Berk with a business proposition.

The Lotte Berk Method, the name Bach selected for her new business venture, launched in the Upper East Side of New York City in 1971. 'I made up the name to honour her . . .' (Bach, 2020).

The programme was well-received in the United States, and Bach was excited to share her success with Berk. However, Berk's reaction was unexpected:

The big step was making that name. I flew her [Berk] to New York. It was a simple place but with lockers and showers, because in New York City they [clients] had to go to work . . . She was so angry about the premises. She did something absolutely terrible. She went out with a group of my clients and talked against me very badly. I never saw her again. (Bach, 2018)

In the United States, Bach further explored ways to modify Berk's methodology to cater to the American marketplace. In 1973, when Bach was approached by Random House to write an exercise book, she proposed calling her book, *The Lotte Berk Method.* Random House rejected the title because the name 'Lotte Berk' was unknown in the United States at that time (Bach, 2018), despite her success in London. As an alternative, Bach named her first book *Awake! Aware! Alive! Exercises for a Vital Body* (Bach, 1973), a name chosen by Bach for its alignment with her Buddhist beliefs.

Details of Bach's exercise modifications and how they affected the evolution of Lotte Berk's innovation will be explored further in Chapters 2 and 3. Bach's sports-focused orientation unquestionably sent Berk's programme, as practiced by Bach, onto a fitness trajectory as opposed to the dance focus that had always been a hallmark of Berk's methodology.

In 1980, Bach hired Halfpapp and Fred DeVito to oversee the Lotte Berk Method as she began to divide her residency between New York City and India. For twenty-two years, Halfpapp—a former ballet dancer who was also an associate in dance education with the Hartford Ballet—served as vice president for the Lotte Berk Method studios, and Fred DeVito—who held a Bachelor of Science in Physical Education and Health from The College of New Jersey—served as director. As Berk's programme continued to evolve in the United States under their direction, Halfpapp and DeVito solidified an American methodology integrating yoga, Pilates, and ballet, which would become known as Barre.

During Bach's visits to India, she began to expand on the way that Berk had used music in her popular classes, not only to create an atmosphere, but also to motivate and enhance performance as well as facilitate emotional well-being:

> I wanted them to get to the point of being out of breath in each series, but I also wanted them to leave the studio with a sense of accomplishment and peacefulness. (Bach, 2020)

Halfpapp and Cheshire each reported the way that Berk paired music to specific movements. For example, Berk always paired a particular 'rounded back' abdominal series, which she called 'Round-Back Zorba', to the music of Zorba the Greek because the progression of tempo and volume matched the progression of exercise intensity (Cheshire, 2019; Halfpapp, 2018). Whereas Berk used music to create atmosphere, establish rhythm, and enhance motivation, Bach expanded on this foundation by choreographing her entire class, pairing specific music with different movements, thereby creating a flow from beginning to end:

> ". . . it [Bach's attention to the choreographic details] was practically all consuming because I wanted to work with a lot of tech guys [techno musicians and DJs] and get the sounds and the beats for each exercise and how many minutes for the section. (Bach, 2020)

In India, Bach produced original CDs that she photographed for the researcher (see Figure 1.1). Anecdotally, the designs on each CD were derived from husband Giacomo Argento's oil paintings.

**Figure 1-1 The Lotte Berk Method CDs by Lydia Bach. Photographs courtesy of Lydia Bach**

## How 'Rehabilitative Exercise' Evolved Into 'Barre'

Analysing how Lotte Berk's original programme evolved through the interpretive lens of three different practitioners—Lotte Berk herself, Lydia Bach, and Esther Fairfax—the researcher discerned three different approaches: one dance-focused, one sports-focused, and one focused on the everyday woman.

Berk's original programme was based on her contemporary dance career and rehabilitation for a drug addiction (Fairfax, 2017; Berk & Prince, 1978). A spinal injury sustained while teaching class, which occurred *after* the origination of the programme, was used as a pretext for Berk's innovation because she was loathe to divulge the facts of her addiction.

In the United States, Bach, who was well-versed in athletics, sent Berk's programme onto a sports-focused trajectory. In the United Kingdom, Fairfax translated her mother's programme into an organized, comprehensive, and more widely inclusive programme based on her experience as a wife, mother, psychologist, and teacher—one that would appeal to the everyday woman. These various modifications to the original methodology, Rehabilitative Exercise, set the foundation for the Barre programmes that are practiced in the United States and United Kingdom today.

Berk's and Fairfax's intimate class size of up to ten students (Fairfax, 2010; Cheshire, 2019; Bach, 2019) became the model for 'boutique' studios, while Bach's expansive range of programmes inspired corporate group fitness.

I loved when we had floor after floor and we could really separate beginners, intermediate, and advanced. The fourth level was Extreme Lotte Berk. Members Only. I loved that level, backbends, splits, all kinds of things. But never an injury and that makes me most proud. (Bach, 2018)

Bach's New York studios expanded to Bridgehampton, New York, and Los Angeles, California, while Berk opened another studio on Fulham Road in London, and Fairfax launched her studio in Hungerford, England. Berk was 46 at the time of her innovation and continued to teach on Fulham Road until she approached her 80th birthday. Contemplating her retirement, Berk first offered her studio to Fairfax, who declined, finding Hungerford more suitable to her lifestyle than London (Fairfax, 2010, pp. 170-171). Berk then offered her studio to Lois Complin, Berk's student and muse. Complin is pictured demonstrating the exercises in Berk and Prince's 1978 book. Fairfax talks about the transition:

> Mother's emotions moved through anger, resentment and utter sadness. She couldn't bring herself to leave her studio alone, even after she had given it to Lois. Every morning she would go to one of the classes and pull one of her favourite students out and take her for a coffee. When she wasn't doing this, mother made Lois's life difficult by constantly going around the class and correcting the students or changing the exercises . . . For two years, Lois put up with Lotte's increasingly difficult behaviour in the studio. Eventually the time came when Lois was almost at the breaking point and she decided to sell the studio to a French student [Gay Christie] who excelled in the exercises and was longing to get her hands on it. This new owner began also being kind to mother whenever she appeared. Mother was becoming a raging inferno of feelings and she made even worse trouble than previously in the classes. [Mother used to say to Christie's students] 'The teaching here is awful. Don't come here again'. (Fairfax, 2010, pp. 261-263)

At first Berk's eccentricities may have overshadowed her declining health. Fairfax noted in her 2010 book:

> We always went to the loo together and I noticed, not for the first time, that she no longer washed her hands but instead sprayed them with perfume, rubbing them together as if with soap. I put it down to her becoming more eccentric now that she was in her eighties and that was only to be expected . . . the next weekend as we sat once again for coffee at Café Rouge, she announced that she would like to move to Hungerford. I was aghast. (Fairfax, 2010, p. 292)

In June 1998, Berk moved into an assisted-living home in Hungerford, where she was later institutionalized with dementia. Fairfax revealed, '[a]nother year went by, and another, until she couldn't use language at all . . . for nearly five years she had been living like this' (Fairfax, 2010, p. 292). At age 90, Berk passed away.

After Berk's passing, Fairfax's jealous grudge against Bach re-emerged in a targeted media campaign to slander Bach, claiming that Bach stole Berk's name and prospects for international recognition. This became the narrative, which continues to be repeated to the present day:

> How the barre workout was created: German-born dancer who fled the Nazis devised an exercise regimen with moves like the 'love-making position' - but died in anonymity after selling the rights to her own name. (Hopkins, 2018)

> . . . She [Bach] was able to secure the franchising rights to The Lotte Berk Method through a deal with Lottie herself — a move that would ultimately leave Lottie without the ability to use her own name for studios, books, or publishing deals. (Sides, 2021)

> A most attractive blond woman, Lydia Bach, had approached mother saying she wanted to train in her method and open a studio in New York. Mother was dazzled by her attention and constant flattery, as well as finding her American brashness amusing. At the end of the training, she handed mother a large amount of money, in cash. Mother's eyes drank in the sight of so many banknotes and she signed the contract without having it vetted by a lawyer. Mother had signed away all the American and Canadian rights for her exercises. Lydia opened a huge studio in Manhattan, as well as one in Los Angeles, and all for the sum of $7,000 a year until mother's death. Later, when mother realized what she had done and wanted to change this contract, lawyers couldn't break it. What really hurt mother was having to turn down offers for books and videos from the States. All the fame could have been hers, though at least her name was still attached to Lydia's studios. (Fairfax, 2010, pp. 208, 209)

When questioned by the researcher, Bach revealed that she was unaware of Fairfax's remarks in the media (Bach, 2018).

While fact-checking claims made by Bach and Fairfax during their interviews, the researcher consulted the United States Patent and Trademark Organization (USPTO) for ownership of the Lotte Berk Method trademark, since this was Fairfax's point of contention—that Bach stole her mother's name. Interestingly, the USPTO documents a first-time registration on 19 July 2004, eight months following Berk's passing, in the name of Bach's attorney of record, Gloria Tsui-Yip (see Appendix A). According to USPTO law, Berk could have registered her own name in the United States during her lifetime, had she chosen to. Furthermore, Fairfax could have done so upon her mother's passing, had she investigated the laws. In fact, the researcher learned during her investigations in 2018 that Berk's name was available for registration in both the United Kingdom and European Union (See Appendix B). In 2005, a year following Berk's passing, Bach closed her studios.

The closing of Bach's studios seeded the Barre industry in the United States, as several of her former teacher employees opened their own private studios and/or corporate franchises. Halfpapp and DeVito had already left Bach's employ in 2003, at which time they produced a teacher training manual entitled *Barre Fitness* TT, which set the precedent for naming the methodology derived from Rehabilitative Exercise as 'Barre' (Halfpapp, 2019). This manual, though produced in the United States, appears to be the first Barre manual in direct lineage from Berk. A subsequent manual was published in the United Kingdom in 2016 by Fairfax, Kenna, and Mimi Whee, a visiting international student in Fairfax's home studio. These manuals are very different in structure, content, methodology, terminology, and target market—differences that will be further detailed in Chapters 2 and 3.

Berk never taught outside the United Kingdom, and her only visit to the United States was as Bach's guest in the early 1970s to see the newly-opened Lotte Berk Method studio. In 2017, at the age of 82, Fairfax made her first visit to the United States and conducted a class in New York City to an intimate group of Barre enthusiasts by invitation of the researcher in partnership with the marketing agency 3DPR (Fairfax, *Lotte Berk's Daughter Talks,* 'Angels Do Exist', 2017).

**Figure 1-2 Esther Fairfax, New York City — Viewership 3,158,697 Self Magazine (online), 2017**

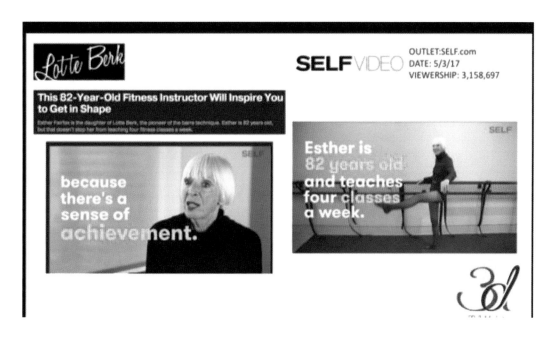

Fairfax retired from teaching toward the end of 2020; and Bach, now in her early 80s, teaches privately from her residences in New York, India, and Jamaica. In addition, Bach is an advocate for worker's rights, animal welfare, and education in underdeveloped countries.

> 'Berk's programme was revolutionary at the time . . . and her exercises really did work!' (Waterloo, 2019).

# Chapter 2.     Barre of the Present
# Current Applications and Future Potential

**How is Barre currently being used and what are potential future applications?**

> I would be really interested in how Barre has variously developed . . . We did
> classes at Barre 3 in Toronto and it wasn't anything like Lotte, so there are lots of
> variations! (Cheshire, 2019)

Barre of the present continues to grow in popularity and evolve as a leading fitness trend (Saedi, 2015; London, 2015; MacVean, 2015; Travers, 2019; Thomason, 2019). In higher education, Barre programmes are offered at universities in the United States, such as Harvard, Notre Dame, University of California–Los Angeles (UCLA) and Purdue, among others; and in the United Kingdom, including Cambridge, Durham University, University of Manchester, University of Bedfordshire, University of Glasgow, and the University of St. Andrews, through their departments of physical education, health and wellbeing, and humanities. Barre classes today are widely discussed in magazine articles, blogs, and a plethora of Barre videos found on the internet. But for all the media attention, this is the first academic investigation of Barre.

Today's Barre programmes have expanded in structure and content from the time of Berk's innovation, the evolution of which, through Bach and Fairfax, set the course for a wide variety of present-day Barre formats. However, it is the researcher's experience in training teachers that today's Barre instructors are often unfamiliar with Berk, her history, and her programme, which was based on contemporary dance. This is evidenced in the structure and content of current programmes that are often unrecognisable when compared with Berk's. This underlines the need for academic investigation to record the original purpose, principles, structure, and content around which Barre was created.

Halfpapp and Cheshire describe Berk's original methodology through its class structure, reporting that the programme's progression initiated with a choreographed warm-up that was followed by exercises targeting anatomical muscle groups: '. . . thigh work, glutes, [abdominal sequences in] flat back, round back, curl . . . that ended with a cool-down section and stretches' (Halfpapp, 2019; Cheshire, 2020).

In Fairfax's 2016 manual, which she referred to in the 2017 interview as 'the Technique', she does not always group the exercises together anatomically, nor does she adhere to the ballet class structure of dividing the class into a standing barre practise followed by floor exercises in the second half. For example, in Fairfax's technique, the standing thigh sequences are followed by a kneeling then a seated series, after which there is a return to the barre for exercises that again target the thighs. Her manual speaks to the programme's user-friendly approach as evidenced by the content's vocabulary, which is devoid of dance pedagogy, anatomical terminology, and Berk's risqué exercise names:

> Warm-up, Legs Side Barre, Face Barre – Bottoms, Backs of Thighs, Side Barre – Outside Thighs, Kneeling Facing Barre, Sit in Centre, All Fours, Back to The Barre, Serious Thighs, Spine/Leg Stretching, Feet Under the Barre, Sardines [crunches], Sit Against the Wall (Part 1), Sit Against the Wall – No Escape (Part 2), Lie On Stomach (Bottoms & Back of Thighs), Arch & Hollow, Footsie Footsie, Sit Legs Apart, Stretch, Give a Gift, Sit Legs Together, Mini Tilt & Touch Toes, Final Spinal Stretch. (Fairfax, Kenna, & Whee, 2016)

Halfpapp and DeVito's 2013 manual, *TT Barre Certified by exhale®* (*TTBC*) varies from Fairfax's in the way that the exercises progress; however, both manuals demonstrate Barre's progression further into the field of fitness and away from Berk's dance focus. An excerpt from *TTBC* illustrates this assertion:

> Warmup, Plank + Upper Body, First Barre Stretch, Thighs, Leg Stretch Series, Gluteal, Prone Gluteal Strengthener, Flat Back [abdominal exercise position], Round Back [abdominal exercise position], Pullups, Curl [abdominal exercise position], Prone Back Strengtheners, Pelvic Tilt, Savasana + Final Stretches. (DeVito & Halfpapp, 2013)

In addition to its structure, the *TTBC* manual employs the content and terminology commonly used in dance, yoga, and Pilates. This manual, which was developed in the United States, also includes detailed anatomical drawings and recommendations for the use of music, verbal cues, and other practical instructions for teachers, including tactile correction suggestions. While these practises are commonly employed in Barre training in the United States (Rosenstein & Arkin, 2014; DeAnda et al., 2016; DeVito & Halfpapp, 2013, 2015), this information is not found in Barre manuals or dance training books in the United Kingdom that were reviewed by the researcher (Fairfax, Kenna, & Whee, 2016; Berk & Prince, 1978; Danby, 1984, 1993; Association of Russian Ballet and Theatre Arts pamphlets).

Today's Barre and its varied programmes are considered fitness regimens. The aspects of art that inspired and underpinned Berk's innovation have mostly been sidelined for the repetitious fitness-exercise component of her original programme. As discussed in Chapter 1, the history of Barre in the current literature focuses on Berk's salacious character and celebrity clientele, and lacks in critical investigation of her methodology, its connection to dance, and its beneficial claims. However, from the time of Berk's innovation to Barre of the present, there has been a surge in empirical studies in dance and sports sciences and in the field of cognition that examines the effects of dance on the brain. These current empirical investigations provide a means for advancing a discussion of Barre and its potential benefits for the performing arts in higher education and beyond.

***What does the current research say about the need for supplemental fitness in dance training?***

> The formal dance class has long been the cornerstone of training, providing all the technical, physical, and aesthetic requirements of dance. This means that training methods, which are generally based on tradition, are not sufficient to help prepare dancers for the higher, more physically demanding aspects of performance. (Irvine, Redding, & Rafferty, 2011)

The research categorises the action of classical ballet as high-intensity and intermittent—two factors which do not necessarily lead to the high level of aerobic fitness that is required for the demands of onstage performance (Cohen, 1985; Cohen et al., 1980, 1982; Allen & Wyon, 2008; Angioi et al., 2009; Wyon et al., 2007). In the investigations, dancers commonly reported less than maximal performance as a result of fatigue. The dancers also reported their belief that fatigue led to their injuries (Baldari & Guidetti, 2001; Allen & Wyon, 2008; Laws, 2005). The findings in the empirical investigations point to the lack of fitness elements in the dancer's practise that would effectively prepare them for the physiological demands of onstage performance, suggesting that it is time to completely rethink the dance class traditions and methodologies. This assertion will be further explored in Chapter 3.

The current literature focuses on the intermittent, stop/start action of the dance practise, with its emphasis on skill acquisition and the artistic aspects of classical and contemporary ballet. The studies scientifically explore the effects of the dancer's daily regimen in relationship to the physiological demands of performance by using diagnostic measurements that range from oxygen intake and lactic acid blood levels to 3D motion capture systems that use reflective markers to analyse physical stress factors (Baldari & Guidetti, 2001; Wyon et al., 2004; Redding et al., 2009). A 2004 study by Yiannis *Koutedakis and* Athanasios *Jamurtas* elucidates this relationship:

… while a normal ballet class elicited a mean lactic acid blood level of 3 mmol/L in women, a choreographed solo part raised it to 10 mmol/L. This value is as high as what top-class football, squash and hockey players achieve during the match. (Koutedakis & Jamurtas, 2004)

In existing sports literature, it is not uncommon to find that some study conclusions contradict others. For example, a once weekly fitness routine that increased leg-press strength in women was found to produce no greater improvements when performed twice weekly (Burt, Wilson, & Willardson, 2007; DiFrancisco-Donoghue & Werner, 2006), while other studies concluded that greater frequency produced greater results (Ralston et al., 2018; Evans, 2019; Schoenfeld, Ogborn, & Krie, 2016). However, in the scientific research on dance, there is a consensus that traditional dance training lacks in the fitness elements of strength and stamina, concluding that dancers need to supplement their daily practise regimen with fitness conditioning not only to maximize performance but also to mitigate or prevent injury (Sandall, 2018; Irvine, Redding, & Rafferty, 2011; Koutedakis et al., 2005; Koutedakis & Sharp, 1999; Clarkson & Skrinar, 1988). The 2011 *Dance Fitness* literature review conducted by the International Association for Dance, Medicine, and Science (IADMS) notes:

In light of these studies, and with increased understanding of the artistic and athletic needs of dancers in different genres, it is no longer acceptable to train dancers without preparing them physiologically for the demands of current choreographic work. (Irvine, Redding, & Rafferty, 2011)

The fitness interventions used in these studies varied widely, and although the studies agreed that supplemental fitness conditioning is necessary, there is no consensus on which fitness programme is most effective:

Dancers use somatic techniques such as Pilates and Gyrotonics as supplemental training, few expose themselves to intensities that will cause strength and cardiorespiratory adaptations. (Irvine, Redding, & Rafferty, 2011)

The researcher proposes that further academic study of Barre methodology may produce additional empirical data to buttress the researcher's assertion that Barre is the fitness conditioning system that would best support the needs of performing artists. Furthermore, the implementation of Barre in higher education, in the very institutions that are at the forefront of research, is precisely the appropriate venue where such a programme could be developed for maximum impact.

*How does the research on dance relate to Barre?*

> . . . in order to achieve efficient and optimal development of dance skills,
> conditioning work over and above daily technique class has been recommended.
> (Irvine, Redding, & Rafferty, 2011)

Many of the studies on dance and dancers describe the way that fitness conditioning can improve physiological capabilities while avoiding negative effects on the art form's aesthetic:

> Improvements in the muscle's ability to generate force seem to be a way for
> dancers to enhance their performance. Soloist ballerinas are characterized, inter
> alia, by increased muscular strength. (Misigoj-Durakovic et al., 2001)

> . . . data on male (Koutedakis et al., 1997) and female (Stalder, Noble, &
> Wilkinson, 1990) ballet dancers revealed that supplemental resistance training for
> hamstrings and quadriceps can lead to improvements in leg strength, without
> interfering with key artistic and physical performance requirements. This supports
> earlier findings where significant muscle strength increases were not accompanied
> by proportional changes in muscle size (MacDougall et al., 1980) and reinforces
> the belief that resistance training is followed by changes within the nervous
> system, which play an active role in strength development. An elevated neural
> involvement may account for some of the exercise-induced increases in muscular
> strength (Ploutz et al., 1985) suggesting that, at least in the early stages of such
> training, hypertrophy is not a prerequisite for strength gains. (Koutedakis &
> Jamurtas, 2004)

Specificity and the use of repetition found in fitness and dance practises are commonly known to be used in Barre (Rosenstein & Arkin, 2014; DeAnda et al., 2016; DeVito & Halfpapp, 2013, 2015, 2019). Moreover, this use of specificity in Barre practise can be tailored to target muscles in the legs in both parallel (adduction) and turned-out (abduction) foot/leg positions; whereas other dance practises, such as ballet, use predominately only one foot/leg position. In the researcher's practical experience, conditioning that combines both adduction and abduction leads to an overall increase of physiological strength and stability.

The effect of fitness conditioning on the aesthetics of classical ballet are investigated in the scientific dance and sports research literature. The study 'Do Increases in Selected Fitness Parameters Affect the Aesthetic Aspects of Classical Ballet Performance?' (Twitchett et al., 2011) states that:

> . . . it has been found that the work that classical ballet dancers carry out in class,
> rehearsal, and performance places little stress on the cardiovascular system and is
> insufficient to further develop aerobic fitness. Furthermore, this extra training was

not detrimental to the dancers and is further evidence to support that the inclusion of a weekly fitness training session into current dance training programmes is enough to cause observable improvements in dancers' artistic abilities. (Twitchett et al., 2011)

In the fitness industry, cardiovascular conditioning is a methodical, well-touted component which has been adapted to signature Barre programmes, such as Cardio Barre, Beachbody, Gold Barre, Barre 3, and Pure Barre, among many others. Barre's adaptability to various conditioning objectives suggests its potential as a uniquely beneficial fitness regimen for dance and beyond.

In pursuit of deeper insight into this question of how Barre can be used and adapted to meet the needs of the performing arts in higher education and beyond, the researcher embarked on a mission to speak with experts and leaders in various fields, including medicine, education, performing arts, dance and sports science, resort health and wellness programmes, and fitness. This opportunity was funded by a generous award through ICURe (Innovation to Commercialisation of University Research), under the auspices of the Directorate of Research and Enterprise (R&E) at Queen's University, Belfast, in collaboration with the universities of Bath, Bristol, Exeter, Southampton, and Surrey.

**The ICURe Interviews**

> As a university, we're about more than just making the next pot of money. We're looking for things that are good for people, that are interesting, that have societal benefit, that have environmental impact, and can make people's lives better. (Wiggins, 2020, *The High Barre* documentary)

Before embarking on the global travel agenda to interview various experts and professionals, a three-day training intensive was held in London to prepare the researcher for the data collection process. The training centred around the workbook *Value Proposition Design,* which offered useful considerations to help identify interview subjects and create questions for interviewees that would elicit insightful information about 'gains' [what was working] and 'pains' [what was not working] within their industry. The workbook further outlined a system for recording the information and identifying trends and recurring themes that would later provide a framework for synthesizing the information.

The researcher travelled for meetings to several cities throughout Italy, the United States, England, Scotland, Germany, Sweden, and Hong Kong. The interviewees who participated in one-to-one meetings with the researcher included (in order of interview):

- Dr Luigi Cucchi, Giornalista e Direttore, Il Giornale, Milan, Italy

- Gianluca Schiavoni, Ballet Dancer and Choreographer, Teatro alla Scala; and Chiara Schiavoni, Ballet Dancer, Teatro alla Scala, Milan, Italy

- Serap Mesutogeu, Guest Relations, Four Seasons Hotels and Resorts, Milan, Italy

- Dr Roberto Pozzoni, Specialista Ortopedia e Traumatologia, Milan, Italy

- Elena Cervellati, Associate Professor, Arts Department, University of Bologna, Italy

- Rocco Di Michele, Associate Professor, Department of Biomedical and Neuromotor Sciences, University of Bologna, Italy

- Felice Limosani, Multidisciplinary Artist, and Doris Anna Kovacs, Libero Professionista, Florence, Italy

- Jamie Harris, Director/Agent, Clear Talent Group, New York, New York, United States

- Carol Espel, Fitness and Program Director, Pritikin Longevity Center and Spa, New York, New York, United States

- Dr Kimberly Chandler Vaccaro, Associate Professor of Dance, Rider University, Ewing, New Jersey, United States

- Emily Bakemeier, Deputy Provost Yale University, New Haven, Connecticut, United States

- James Bundy, Dean of the Yale School of Drama and Artistic Director of Yale Repertory Theatre, New Haven, Connecticut, United States

- Todd Lanman, MD, Spinal Neurosurgeon, Los Angeles, California, United States

- Jonas Wright, Dean and Chief Academic Officer of the San Francisco Conservatory of Music, California, United States

- Tak Friedman and Terry Berg, Wellness Team, Rosewood Resort, Hong Kong, China

- William Baugh, The Tina Turner Musical, Hamburg, Germany

- Dr Susan Kozel, Professor of Philosophy, Dance and Media Technologies, Malmo University, Sweden

- Margaret Morris Movement, West Sussex, United Kingdom

- Catherine Cassidy, Director, and Lisa Sinclair, Dance Health Manager, The Scottish Ballet, Glasgow, Scotland, United Kingdom

- Chrissy Delapperall, Manager Virgin Active, Chelmsford, United Kingdom

- Dr Emma Redding, Head of Dance Science, Trinity Laban Conservatoire of Music and Dance, London, United Kingdom

- Dr Marcus Dunn, Research Fellow, Centre of Sports Engineering Research, Sheffield Hallam University, Sheffield, United Kingdom

After arriving at each destination, the researcher reviewed the expert's biography and focus of their research or professional career, confirmed the location of the meeting, and created a list of questions for the interviewee. During their interviews, the experts conversed about their professional experience and concerns, often responding to questions prepared in advance, or conversing freely, sharing information without being prompted. The researcher took notes which were completed and stored before travelling to the next appointment. It is important to note that the ICURe training specifically instructed the researcher not to evaluate or judge the information gathered during the data collection phase.

Following the three-month interview process, the researcher then attended a final training intensive back in London to analyse and synthesise the information collected in order to begin evaluating the potential for present-day and future Barre programmes. All information gathered during the data collection phase was subjected to critical analysis, over the course of several months, for the purpose of validating the veracity of each expert's statements.

### *What the experts discussed in their interviews*

The process of analysis revealed shared areas of concern, regardless of the expert's field or area of expertise. These concerns were tabulated according to the frequency that they arose during the three-month interview time period. The process of identifying common themes and tallying the number of experts who shared these specific concerns produced the following list: 1) physical and mental injury; 2) weight issues; 3) lack of movement opportunities; 4) education of teachers; 5) process-based versus product-based learning; 6) career transitions for retiring professional performing artists; and 7) programmes for injury prevention. Highlighted below are discussion points from interviews that produced the most illustrative synopsis of each particular concern.

### Physical and Mental Injury

Each of the interviewees highlighted their concerns about injuries in their field or workplace.

James Bundy, Dean of the Yale School of Drama, reported that physical injuries were a significant problem in his department to the extent that he initiated an assessment of other university acting programmes for comparison. During his interview, Bundy discussed a national injury problem among performing artists that he attributed to "over-energized nerves" and theatrical high-energy action that often included stage props.[1]

During critical analysis of the literature, the researcher found that the subject of injury in the arts has been widely studied. Numerous surveys document the mental and physical challenges faced by performing artists and theatre workers, including voice strain, musculoskeletal problems, concussions, and broken bones[2] (Ackermann & Bronner, 2019; Bailey, 2018; Evans, Evans, & Carvajal, 1996, 1998). Moreover, the resources associate these injuries with a number of factors, including costuming, special effects and lighting, backstage conditions, stage sets or raked stages[3] and actors who are not fit enough to meet the physical demands of their roles (Kloberdanz, 2020). Surveys of performing artists on Broadway and London's West End identified an 'extensive rate of injuries': in Broadway productions and touring companies, 55% of all performers were found to have sustained at least one injury which was comparable to the findings of West End performers that found 46% of performers had sustained injuries (Evans, Evans, & Carvajal, 1996, 1998; Kloberdanz, 2020). The 2018 Ohio State University study, 'High number of concussion-related symptoms in performing arts', found a high incidence of concussion among workers in the performing arts, notably '67 percent of theatre workers surveyed have experienced head impacts and 39 percent had more than five' (Russell & Daniell, 2018). Fortunately, fatal theatre injuries are uncommon (Kloberdanz, 2020).

Jonas Wright, Dean and Chief Academic Officer of the San Francisco Conservatory of Music (SFCM), expressed concern about injuries, both mental and physical, in the school. He disclosed that a student enrolled in the programme had attempted suicide the week prior. His conversation did not divulge details of the student or circumstances; however, it was clear that

---

[1] Theatrical properties, or 'props', are objects used by the performing artist to enhance the realism of staged scenes.
[2] "Musculoskeletal (MSK) conditions affect the joints, bones and muscles, and also include rarer autoimmune diseases and back pain," according to the National Health Service (NHS). Musculoskeletal disorders include: carpal tunnel syndrome, tendonitis, muscle/tendon strain, tension neck syndrome, thoracic outlet compression, rotator cuff tendonitis, epicondylitis, radial tunnel syndrome, digital neuritis, trigger finger/thumb, DeQuervain's syndrome, mechanical back syndrome, degenerative disc disease, ruptured/herniated disc, and many more. (Argo Plus) Frequently used in Elizabethan times as well as in theaters of the nineteenth century, a raked stage is one that is built on an angle that slopes upward and away from the front the stage. (Causey, 2019)
[3] Frequently used in Elizabethan times as well as in theaters of the nineteenth century, a raked stage is one that is built on an angle that slopes upward and away from the front of the stage. (Causey, 2019)

the school's position was one of compassion and support for the student, who fortunately survived, and to prevent such an occurrence in the future.

The literature confirms that college students in the performing arts are at high risk for mental health issues as a result of stress, competitive pressures, and low self-esteem (Wainwright, Williams, & Turner, 2005; Evans, Evans, & Carvajal, 1996, 1998; Kloberdanz, 2020). Moreover, research studies associate physical and mental problems in the performing arts with substance abuse. A study of university dancers and theatre performers found that in the 30 days prior to the survey, 28 percent reported the use of tobacco, 12 percent had used marijuana, 71 percent had consumed alcohol, 18 percent reported other drug use, and 7 percent used drugs for performance enhancement (Werner, 1991). A study of the International Conference of Symphony and Opera Musicians (ICSOM) found that 27 percent had used propranolol, or some other beta blocker, before every orchestral performance, and in 70 percent of its use, the drug was obtained without a doctor's prescription (Tindall, 2004; Werner, 1991; Descoteaux, 2014; Kloberdanz, 2020; Beder, 2016). The Musician's Health Collective study, 'Beta-blockers, performance anxiety, and the results of the musicians' health survey', suggested that 79 percent of musicians had tried beta blockers to enhance performance (Beder, 2016).

Overuse is another cause of injury to performing artists, due to the early age at which formal training often begins.

Carol Espel, Fitness and Program Director, Pritikin Longevity Center and Spa, discussed 'overuse syndromes'[4] and her injuries, attributing them to early musical theatre training which resulted in double hip replacements by the age of 40. Another expert, Jamie Harris, director of Clear Talent Group, a bi-coastal talent agency, stated that dancers often have a short 'dance-life' due to injuries that end their performing careers in their early 30s. Harris agreed with Espel that the prevalence of overuse injuries in the performing arts is also due to training practises, such as turnout (the position of the legs/feet in ballet), which have repercussions down the road.

Gianluca Schiavoni, a choreographer, actor, dancer at the Teatro alle Scala Academy and graduate of La Sapienza University in Literature and Philosophy, discussed turnout in classical ballet as a source of injury, and expressed his concern that career success often depended to a certain extent on this aesthetic. Gianluca further observed that in order to achieve the idealized

---

[4] The symptom complexes defined as injuries caused by the cumulative effects on tissues of repetitive physical stress that exceeds physiologic limits (Werner, 2009).

180-degree turned-out position, dancers compensated by arching their backs—'belly out'—which he said 'caused injuries to nearly everyone in the company'.

A study of particular interest, conducted in collaboration with the Royal Opera House in London, found that 'dancers suffer an injury rate comparable to American football, with a mean of 6.8 injuries per year' (Bailey, 2018; Werner et al., 2009). In another study, all participants (20 dancers) were found to have sustained injuries, finding that 'the injured, dancing body is perceived as an inevitable part of a career in ballet . . . on a more everyday level, dancing and performing with painful, niggling injuries is the norm' (Wainwright, Williams, & Turner, 2005).

According to Dr Roberto Pozzoni, *Specialista in Ortopedia e Traumatologic* [Specialist in Orthopaedics and Trauma], who specialises in treating elite athletes, dancers, and footballers,[5] his patients commonly suffer overuse injuries or trauma as a result of impact during performance. Dr Pozzoni's primary concerns were injury prevention and post-surgical rehabilitation, 'getting footballers back into the game quicker and stronger'.

Research studies on footballers find many similarities to studies focusing on dancers, in which 82.9 percent of injuries sustained are commonly to the lower extremities (Stubbe et al., 2015; Ekstrand, Hagglund, & Walden, 2011).

Spinal neurosurgeon Todd Lanman, MD, one of the leading surgeons in the United States, reported that his patients were most often injured as a result of everyday occurrences, such as sneezing and coughing. However, he related overuse injuries to sports in which hyperextension of the spine is common, such as aerobic gymnastics, dance, and weight lifting. Lanman was also concerned about weight- and age-related spinal injury. When asked for advice on injury prevention, Lanman replied, 'stay lean and stay strong'.

The literature on lumbar disk herniation (LDH) confirmed that the common causation for injuries resulted from coughing or sneezing. The studies further suggested hereditary factors in addition to 'inciting events', such as lifting, sports, daily living tasks, and accidents (Viikari-Juntura, Martikinen, & Riihimaki, 2002; Videman et al., 1997, 2007, 2010).

---

[5] The Oxford Dictionary describes footballer as a person who plays soccer; a soccer player.

**Weight Issues**

Within the general reporting of weight issues, there were two overlapping concerns: the effects of weight in relationship to the occurrence of injury and the relationship between weight and physical exercise.

Serap Mesutogeu, Director of Guest Relations at the Four Seasons Hotel in Milan, Italy, expressed her concern about the sedentary nature of her workplace, not only for herself but also for her colleagues. While concerned about the effects of job-specific overuse in housekeeping and guest services, her greater concern centred around the weight gain that resulted from prolonged physical inactivity due to computer use, a fundamental job requirement.

Consistent with Mesutogeu's observations, research studies connected a sedentary workplace and lifestyle to the likelihood of weight gain. Moreover, scientific studies on Body Mass Index (BMI) link sedentary lifestyles with high BMI [being overweight], a factor shown to have deleterious health effects (Lin et al., 2015; Hu et al., 2003; Patel et al., 2010). A 2009–2010 Center for Disease Control (CDC) study showed that obesity affected 78 million adults in the United States, and that obesity increased the incidence of high blood pressure (hypertension), type 2 diabetes, coronary heart disease, stroke, gallbladder disease, osteoarthritis (breakdown of cartilage/bone in the joint), many types of cancer, low quality of life, mental illness, anxiety, body pain, and physical dysfunctions (Center for Disease Control (CDC); Ogden et al., 2012; Finkelstein et al., 2009; Jensen & Ryan, 2013; Bhaskaran, 2014; Kasen, 2008; Roberts, 2003). Obese patients are reported to have 46 percent higher inpatient costs, 27 percent more physician visits, higher outpatient costs, and 80 percent increased spending on prescription drugs, totalling an estimated $147 billion in the United States in 2008. In 2014, a population-based cohort study of more than 5 million adults in the United Kingdom also found that being overweight or obese was linked to the prevalence of 17 types of cancer (Bhaskaran et al., 2014; Kasen, 2008; Roberts, 2003).

Dean Jonas Wright spoke to the increasing weight of the students and his observation of their 'bad meal choices' in the school's dining areas. His concerns mirrored findings that obesity is becoming an epidemic according to The World Health Organization (WHO):

> … [T]he adult disease burden is due to health risk behaviours that start during adolescence … It has been shown that after the transition from adolescence to young adulthood, when independency increases, young adults are continuously

challenged to make healthful food choices. Along with unhealthy eating behaviours, a new series of weight-related behavioural patterns begins throughout this period, such as excessive alcohol consumption and a low level of physical activity. (Sogari et al., 2018; World Health Organization, 2018)

At the Teatro alla Scala in Milan, Gianluca and his wife, Chiara Schiavoni, noted problems resulting from the opposite extreme of the BMI scale. Chiara reported a diet of one apple and yogurt per day from age 14 to 20. In conversation, Chiara reflected on how her stringent dieting affected her physical health, its negative impact on the longevity of her classical ballet career, and the resulting injuries that later required surgery. The literature on classical ballet dancers widely documents the impact of dietary restrictions on female dancers and the body's inability to repair itself. Female dancers are known to experience amenorrhea (menstrual irregularity), which becomes more serious over time as oestrogen plays a role in maintenance of tissues and organs in the body. Moreover, amenorrhea is found to negatively affect bones, the cardiovascular system, and the dancer's mental well-being (Shufelt, Torbari, & Dutra, 2017; Werner, 1991; Solomon & Perkins, 1989; Lardieri, 2018):

> Injury, and anorexia inclusive, is therefore inherent to the world of young ballerinas and part of their habitus. It is rarely regarded by peers, teachers or choreographers as pathology but rather as body-modification and perfection for dancing. (Gvion, 2008)

The research also discusses the dichotomy between the wellness of dancers and their professional identity in an art form that finds the ultra-thin body to be more highly esteemed by the audience and the professional ballet community. The research clearly shows the need for nutritional counselling in the performing arts and in sports, such as running and gymnastics, that promote thinness (Gvion, 2008; Wainwright, Williams, & Turner, 2007; York-Pryce, 2014; Willard & Lavallee, 2016; Muzaffar, 2014).

## Lack of Movement Programmes

Interviewees in the United States reported a lack of participation in movement programmes due to lack of time and the prohibitive cost of fitness clubs, memberships, and/or personal trainers. In Europe, the interviewees responded that physical exercise wasn't 'part of their culture', and therefore, fitness programmes weren't easily accessible.

Dr Luigi Cucchi, director of the Milan-based newspaper *Il Giornale,* who introduced the practice of highlighting the latest news and research in various sectors, such as education, sports, arts, travel, automotive, and health, discussed his interest in social activities that promoted exercise. However, he stated that ultimately such programmes were difficult to find or access because '[exercising] is not part of the Italian culture'.

In Bologna, Elena Cervelatti, a dance journalist, researcher, and Associate Professor in the Department of the Arts at the Università di Bologna (UNIBO), spoke to the difficulty of participating in physical activities as a matter of accessibility. She explained that the university does not offer dance or stage movement practises in its curriculum and noted that when the university was established in 1088, study of the arts focused on philosophical underpinnings and was not designed for more practical, professional career development. Cervelatti's students have customarily attended academies outside UNIBO to practise their chosen art form; however, she stated that increasing demand from students will eventually lead to changes within the arts curriculum: 'Italy is slow to make change, but it will happen'.

In 2014, the Eurobarometer, a series of public opinion surveys conducted regularly on behalf of the European Commission, reported that 60 percent of people in Italy do not participate in any sport or exercise programmes, and 50 percent do not participate in other physical activities, such as gardening and dancing. The Eurobarometer study highlighted time constraints, lack of interest, and programme expense as reasons for not engaging in physical exercise or activity.

In New York City, Jamie Harris, a former musical theatre performer, reported that his professional lifestyle presented scheduling challenges as an obstacle to taking dance classes, his preferred choice of exercise. Whereas, Emily Bakemeier, Deputy Provost and Dean of Faculty Affairs at Yale University, found that scheduling a personal trainer in advance allowed her to maintain a daily fitness regimen and that alternating her routine between Pilates reformer,[6] Gyrotonics,[7] swimming, and running (which she reported doing less with age) kept her motivated.

---

[6] The Pilates reformer is a popular apparatus designed by Joseph Pilates which consists of a moving carriage within a frame, a system of springs and leverages for resistance while performing strength conditioning targeting specific muscle groups.

[7] Gyrotonic is a unique system of exercise that incorporates movement principles from yoga, dance, gymnastics, swimming and t'ai chi. Central to gyrotonic is the Gyrotonic Expansion System, or GXS, a specially designed wooden machine with rotational discs and weighted pulleys that allow the exerciser to strengthen their muscles using flowing, circular movements. (Hall, Joanna, 2007)

At the time of Dean Bundy's interview, Yale, like UNIBO and many of the leading performing arts programmes in the United Kingdom, offered no movement classes accompanied by music in their departments—although the San Francisco Conservatory of Music and Yale School of Drama do offer Alexander Technique,[8] stage combat, and clowning courses in their curricula.

**Education of Teachers**

The interviewees in the education sector voiced their concern for teachers keeping 'current' and continuing the process of up-skilling their own professional practises. Both Dean Bundy and Dean Wright discussed how essential it is for high-calibre educators to have the ability to mentor students while also being distinguished in their own professions. Dean Wright also highlighted his philosophy that performing arts students needed to be educated as future teachers, a point he regularly makes in his welcoming speech to prospective candidates at the school (SFCM).

The study 'What Makes a Good Teacher?' divides the 'good teacher's' characteristics into two parts: (1) personality traits, and (2) abilities, skills, and professional competencies (Zagyvane, 2017). The studies and surveys of high-level performing arts faculty members in higher education reported that 66 percent of them agreed that their performing career was vital to their teaching practises, stating that it nurtured their ability to successfully mentor students (Haldane, 2018; Bennett & Steinberg, 2006; Brinck, 2018).

At the Virgin Active fitness club in Chelmsford, England, manager Chrissy Delapperall reported her company's Rock Star education programme is designed to support the creative potential of their top-tier instructors. Discussing the business impact of excellent instruction to the success of the clubs, she stated:

> Group fitness classes are the biggest attraction and retention tool. A popular class can increase an hour in the club by 40 percent; and on a Sunday morning, that's 30 more swipes [membership card entry] into the club by adding one new class. (Delapperall, 2019)

---

[8] Alexander Technique is named after the innovator Australian Frederick Matthias Alexander (1869-1955). It is process that teaches how to properly coordinate body and mind to release harmful tension and improve posture, coordination and general health.

In addition to good instruction benefiting learners, good teachers generate revenue for educational institutions and commercial enterprises. The global fitness and health club industry generated more than $96 billion (US) in revenue in 2019 (Gough, 2021).

## Process- versus Product-Based Learning

Over the course of several interviews in the United States, the educational philosophy of 'process- versus product-based learning' emerged as a theme in higher education circles. Deans Bundy and Wright used this term verbatim when discussing the underpinnings of their respective programmes. Pietor Toth defines this philosophy in his educational blog post, 'Knowledge Building: A Process to Understanding your Learning Process':

> A process is a series of steps designed to lead to a particular outcome or goal. It is exploration, a journey, it is fluid, dynamic. A product is the outcome or goal of a process. It is static, solid, fixed in a single moment, a snapshot, usually an artifact created through that process. In terms of education, you could say that process is how learning happens and product is what has been learned. How learning happens relates to pedagogy, teaching and learning styles, philosophies, classroom management, etc. The product artifacts could be test results, oral presentations, visual displays, physical or digital models, essays, etc. You get the idea. To use the example of an iceberg, process is the entire iceberg while product is only the tip, the smallest part that is visible above the water line. What we see is the product and not the process that supports it and makes it visible. (Toth, 2018)

Deans Bundy and Wright also used another phrase verbatim: 'meet the student at their level'. At both Yale and SFCM, students advance through their programme via a performance-based process, an assessment method that provides greater latitude for artistic expression, rather than having their work assessed through written exams. Dr Susan Kozel, Professor of Philosophy, Dance and Media Technologies in the School of Arts and Culture at Sweden's Malmo University, also discussed her department's philosophy that the process of performance represents the core of each individual's educational journey.

## Professional Performing Artist Career Transitions

The challenges facing performing artists at career end are well documented (Cascone, 2018; The National Endowment for the Arts, 2019; Muzaffar, 2014; Wainwright, Williams, & Turner, 2005; Willard & Lavallee, 2016). The statistics for dancers and choreographers show that 27 percent are college educated, and that many are forced into early retirement by the age of 35 by a variety of circumstances.

During Harris' interview, he shared the story of his personal transition from musical theatre, with aid from the Actor's Fund. In the United States, two American labour unions, the Screen Actors Guild (SAG) and the American Federation of Television and Radio Artists (AFTRA), represent 160,000 actors, announcers, broadcast journalists, dancers, DJs, news writers, news editors, programme hosts, puppeteers, recording artists, singers, stunt performers, voiceover artists, and other media professionals. These unions support performing artists as they transition from stage to other careers.

Catherine Cassidy, Director of Engagement with the Scottish Ballet, credited the Dancer's Career Development, a UK-based organisation for dancers, with providing retraining grants, support for up-skilling programmes, and networking through partnering organisations. Cassidy also shared that members of the Scottish Ballet were actively involved in teaching classes in their community wellness programmes and that the success of these efforts was financially supporting the dancers-in-residence.

**Injury Prevention Programmes**

At the Four Seasons Hotel in Milan, Italy, Serap Mesutogeu deliberated over programmes for the prevention of overuse injuries amongst staff in various roles. When the outdoor grounds could be used, Mesutogeu offered complementary yoga classes to employees that were tailored to their specific needs.

Will Baugh, opera and musical theatre performer with *The Tina Turner Musical* in Hamburg, Germany, spoke about the subsidized healthcare programmes in Germany for professional performing artists. These programmes support fitness memberships, dance classes, and other self-care costs. Baugh attributed improvement in strength, confidence, mood, and stress levels to regular attendance in these programmes.

Dr Emma Redding, Head of Dance Science at Trinity Laban Conservatoire of Music and Dance, is a leader in the field of research on injury and injury prevention. Redding's laboratory is equipped with real-time monitors to analyse the effects of dance on lactic acid levels, balance, and oxygen intake. Trinity Laban also offers health and injury support through complementary sessions in Pilates, yoga, and Alexander Technique. Furthermore, Dr Redding is a founding partner of the National Institute of Dance Medicine and Science (NIDMS), launched in 2012 to connect dance institutions in the United Kingdom and to promote university research. The

NIDMS publishes a plethora of research that supports injury prevention programmes, one of which notes that 'a year of [fitness] conditioning can slash the injuries suffered by female dancers from 4.14 per 1,000 hours of dancing to 1.71' (Bailey, 2018; Irvine, Redding, & Rafferty, 2011).

In West Sussex, England, the researcher attended a weekend residential retreat to study the Margaret Morris Movement (MMM) programme, which had been highly recommended for its stratified method designed to accommodate the needs of learners from different backgrounds and dance experience. MMM was founded in 1910 by Margaret Morris, whose innovation combined modern dance movement and dance movement therapy. The researcher found that, overall, the MMM programme of dance variations paired with Morris's original music from the early 1900s was outdated, to its detriment. Prior to attending the retreat, the researcher had been informed that MMM's programme had many similarities to Berk's. However, the teachers trained by Berk continued evolving her methodology, whereas Morris's teachers have continued to adhere to her original programme.

### *What do the ICURe interviews tell us about Barre's potential uses?*

The ICURe interviews offered thought-provoking ideas about Barre's vast potential for various applications. The following graph outlines a number of potential Barre programmes devised in light of these discussions, as well as those developed during the course of doctoral research.

**Figure 2-1 Potential uses for The High Barre programmes in Education, Health and Well-Being, and Fitness**

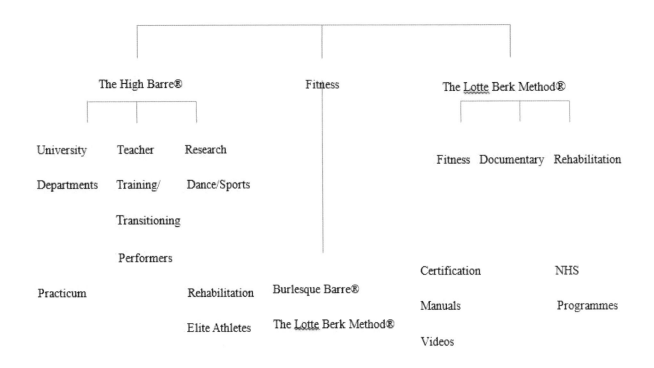

Figure 2.1 illustrates the categories for potential development of Barre programmes: (1) The High Barre® for Higher Education, (2) Fitness applications, and (3) The Lotte Berk Method® for Health and Well-Being. Under the heading of The High Barre, which is intended solely for university educational applications, subcategories include: (a) a programme for university performing arts curricula; (b) a programme for training teachers and transitioning performance artists for careers in education; and (c) a programme to foster Barre vis-à-vis dance/sports science research. The High Barre curriculum would be designed to integrate the study of anatomy, kinesiology, music, and choreography. Additionally, an evaluator training programme would be developed to train traveling evaluators to ensure the integrity of Barre programmes in much the same way as systems used by the Royal Academy of Dance (RAD) and the Association of Russian Ballet and Theatre Arts (ARBTA).

Under the Fitness heading, exercise programmes would be tailored for the fitness industry. Programmes include: (a) Burlesque Barre, (b) the Lotte Berk Method, and (c) Rehabilitative Exercises. Burlesque Barre, an original programme designed by the researcher which integrates jazz dance technique, was launched at the World Barre Summit in 2019, featured in 2020, and is scheduled to be featured again in 2021. The Lotte Berk Method geared for fitness is a derivative of Bach's method that focuses on the core principles of Barre as practised in the United States. Rehabilitative Exercise is based on Berk's original programme as practised in the United Kingdom, inspired by contemporary dance and incorporating spinal rehabilitation exercises.

The Lotte Berk Method geared toward Health and Well-Being is an umbrella for the historic legacy of Lotte Berk, dedicated to the preservation of the original methodologies and rehabilitative aspects of Berk's innovation. Such programmes include, but are not limited to, Barre for special education, the elderly, addiction recovery, and medical interventions under the National Health Service (NHS) or other healthcare systems.

While the above-noted applications represent an array of opportunities for Barre's implementation, it is important to recognise that some of the outlined programmes rely more heavily on Barre's fitness-related aspects and others more on its dance-related aspects. The following chapters will examine both and how they relate to the performing arts in higher education.

# Chapter 3.      Barre for Higher Education: Fitness or Art?

**Why does Barre belong in performing arts curricula in higher education?**

> It's terrific, Jill, that you want to bring Lotte back in her rightful place, not in the
> fitness world, but in the performing arts. I feel quite strongly about this, also
> because I knew my mother's wishes, and mine are the same: the Lotte Berk
> technique, her technique, isn't something that should be in a fitness programme.
> It's saddened me that people have gone all over the world and made some of what
> she does a fitness programme. It's definitely art. It's a performance art. It would
> go so well in a performance art programme. (Fairfax, 2017)

This chapter will focus on Barre and examine what defines a programme as a dance art
form or a fitness regimen. In doing so, the researcher will explore various aspects of dance and
fitness within Barre practise that can be tailored to benefit learners in performing arts
programmes in higher education.

The principles that underpin programmes as art or fitness are complex, although various
aspects of each can be easily identified by the observer. For example, an audience at the ballet
would not be inclined to focus on the fitness elements of the dancer, as neither the fans attending
a tennis match would be evaluating the aesthetics of the game or the artistry of the players. There
is, however, an overlap where aspects of the arts and fitness are commonly recognized to co-
exist, such as in women's gymnastics, figure skating, and synchronized swimming, as well as in
contemporary dance competitions, dance teams, and other dance-fitness genres of today.

In Chapters 1 and 2, the origin and trajectory of Barre are documented in order to
understand how it came to be placed within the context of fitness, though this was not the
primary use Berk intended:

> I don't want to be famous for my exercises. I don't want to be known as a keep-fit
> person. Oh, how I hate those words: keep fit. I want to be known for my creative
> dance, my artistic talents, to be taken seriously as an Artist. (Fairfax, 2010, p. 79)

Berk's knowledge of music and dance, various aspects from her professional performing
career, her recovery from addiction, and a later spinal injury, were integrated into her
methodology. In Berk's daughter's interview with the researcher, Fairfax states that her mother
had already innovated her programme based on dance and was teaching in her studio on
Manchester Street when she slipped a disc stretching a participant in the class—a statement that
supports the claim that rehabilitation for spinal injuries was not the original intention for Berk's

innovation. Fairfax simply states that Berk sought recovery from drug addiction by connecting to her passion for dance and music, and that she was supported by friends and family in doing so:

> . . . [Berk's landlord] offered Lotte a year's rent if she wanted to do something . . . She [Berk] said 'I hate teaching, I'm not a teacher! But I'll do some dancing'. And it evolved . . . She started just running a class . . . That gave mother a chance to start letting it evolve through her love of movement . . .
>
> She [Berk] had slipped a disc. She went to a wonderful German, Jewish doctor because she would be inclined to do that . . . Dr Apple.[9] He showed where you lie flat on your back and you just tilt your pelvis . . . And Lotte immediately thought, 'Woo! I could use that,' but she didn't think of that as part of her new technique. She was doing happily and she just added it. (Fairfax, 2017)

Moreover, Berk's 1978 book defines her programme as a combination of 'modern ballet, yoga and orthopaedics' (Berk & Prince, 1978).

The synthesis of Berk's artistic endeavours and rehabilitative therapy is the hallmark of her programme. This information is important to record as Berk's history, her motivation, and the content of her original programme have become increasingly difficult to locate in the literature, have been lost, or have been previously undocumented. Berk and Prince's 1978 book, as well as books by Berk's affiliate, Lydia Bach, are all long out of print.

Though Berk's programme was considered revolutionary at the time, the combining of fitness and arts principles had been practised for centuries in classical ballet.

**Classical Ballet**

Ballet originated in 1533 with the marriage of Henri II and Catherine de Medici that formed an alliance between the French and Italian courts. Dance spectacles were performed by courtiers and princes in events in which the king would commonly portray himself in the image of Apollo. The aristocracy embodied an idealized posture, elegance, and aesthetic that became associated with ballet. In the 1670s, the positions and steps themselves were codified on behalf of Louis XIV, who engaged Pierre Beauchamp with the task (Homas, 2010). This codification of postures and steps was to become the grammar of ballet that is drawn upon in current dance-fitness programmes such as Barre. Moreover, the heightened use of repetition and extended one-

---

[9] In the book co-authored by Berk and Prince, Dr Guy Beauchamp is identified as the physician responsible for introducing the exercises for Berk's spinal rehabilitation (Berk & Prince, 1978).

legged balances derived from early nineteenth-century classical ballet can be seen in current-day fitness practises whose applications would be beneficial to dance education today.

The 2010 book by Jennifer Homas, *Apollo's Angels: A History of Ballet*, outlines the daily practise regimen of the Danish Bournonville style:

> forty-eight pliés [knee bending exercises], one-hundred and twenty-nine grand battements [large range-of-movement kicks], ninety-seven petits battements [small beating exercises to prepare for jumps in the centre floor where the feet 'beat' in the air] and glissé [gliding exercises for practice of foot articulation], one-hundred and twenty-eight ronds de jambe sur terre [circling the leg on the floor], one-hundred and twenty-eight en l'air [in the air], ending with one-hundred and twenty-eight petits battements sur le-cou-de-pied [small beats with one foot positioned at the ankle]. (Homas, 2010)

*Apollo's Angels* further documents the practise regimen of renowned nineteenth-century ballerina Marie Taglioni, whom the author describes as 'one of the most important and influential ballerinas who ever lived. According to Homas, Taglioni's unpublished memoir records her six-hour daily practise, which the ballerina claims helped her achieve an aura of 'floating' for her role as the Sylph in *La Sylphide*, which she famously performed at the Paris Opera:

> . . . Taglioni further disguised her defects, and increased her range of movement, by developing extraordinary muscle power. When she trained, she held each pose to the count of one hundred—an agonizing challenge for even the strongest dancers today. . . before bed, she worked for an additional two hours (for a total of six hours a day), this time exclusively on jumps. She began with exercises in which she bent her knees, back straight, in *grand plié,* so that she could touch the floor with her hands without leaning over, she pushed herself up to full pointe on the tips of her toes—a move requiring enormous power in the back and legs . . . in subsequent iterations, the push became a jump . . . she repeated all of these exercises many, many times, and they formed the basis for her training for years to come. (Homas, 2010, pp. 139-140)

'Taglioni galvanized a generation and drew some of Europe's best literary minds to dance; she was an international celebrity—ballet's first—and she set the pattern for Margot Fonteyn, Melissa Hayden, Galina Ulanova, and others to follow' (Homas, 2010, pp. 135-36).

Recent examples of ballet training that combines aspects of fitness and dance are found in the description of the late George Balanchine, co-founder and artistic director of the New York City Ballet for more than thirty-five years, who is considered to be the father of the Neoclassical style in American ballet. In articles and books, former members of the New York City Ballet speak to Balanchine's affinity for highly repetitious exercises in his teaching methodology (Homas, 2010, p. 509; Kirkland, 1986):

> So, when Balanchine taught company class, as he did almost daily in the early years, he emphasised clarity and precision—not perfection, necessarily, but the physical geometry of classical ballet. Hours were spent, for example, on fifth position—exactly heel to toe—and *tendus*, hundreds of them, to make the movement (however unnatural) second nature. (Homas, 2010, p. 509)

## 'Luigi' Jazz (Dance)

Another dance style known as jazz was conceived in the 1950s by Eugene Louis Facciuto (20 March 1925 – 7 April 2015), who is often credited as being the 'father of jazz.' Notably, Facciuto's programme was innovated as a means for rehabilitation from injuries he suffered in a car accident.

Eugene Louis Facciuto, who became known as 'Luigi', was a dancer in the American musical films produced by Metro-Goldwyn-Mayer Studios (MGM), where he worked with Gene Kelly. To avoid the confusion of having two same-named artists on set, Kelly took to calling Faccuito by the nickname 'Luigi'. At the age of 21, Luigi was involved in a car accident that left him with paralysis on the right side of his body and the left side of his face—injuries that later required considerable 'warm-up' prior to dancing. Luigi developed a system of exercises that the other dancers on-set took to following. Later in his career, Luigi became a choreographer and teacher to students such as Donna McKechnie, John Travolta, and Liza Minnelli. Luigi's Jazz Centre opened in 1957, and he published his exercise book in 1987.

The researcher was a student of Luigi's for several years in New York City during an apprenticeship with the Harkness Ballet Company and had first-hand knowledge of the exercise system he used to rehabilitate his injuries. Later, during the process of doctoral study, the researcher sought to clarify the conflation of Luigi's and Berk's backgrounds as recorded in Barre manuals and other media sources. Curiously, a former employee from Lydia Bach's studio, Tanya Becker, had been a member of Luigi's performing company. After leaving Bach's employ, Becker became the founder of Physique 57, a Barre franchise that caters to an affluent clientele (Ross, 2012). Because of the somewhat sordid backstory behind Barre's inception, as a means for Lotte Berk to recover from a morphine addiction after ending an adulterous, homosexual relationship—a history that would undoubtedly not have played well for the marketing purposes of a corporate fitness brand—Luigi's story was adapted to become the story of Lotte Berk and the development of her Rehabilitative Exercise. From there, Berk's fabricated history would become the 'official' version that was propagated by the media.

It is notable that Luigi's system of exercises, which was originally conceived as a method of physical therapy, became popular as a form of jazz dance (Facciuto, 1987), while Berk's programme, which was founded on contemporary dance, has been placed in the realm of physical fitness.

**Pilates' Exercise System**

Through Berk's connection to the arts, she sought to rehabilitate herself from despairing circumstances—much like Joseph Pilates did, who created a methodology he called 'Contrology' while incarcerated on the Isle of Man for four years during WWI (September 1915 – March 1919) (Wernick, 1962). In Pilates' words: 'I had plenty of time to invent chairs, beds and exercise equipment . . .' (*Knockaloe.im*). Pilates was released from Camp Knockaloe on the Isle of Man in March 1919, and later resided in Hamburg, Germany, until 1925, where his work branched out into the contemporary dance community and influenced Hanya Holm to create her 'Holm Technique,' which was based on Pilates' system of exercise (Romano & Pont, 2013).

The six years Pilates spent working in Germany after the war would have coincided with Berk's early contemporary dance training in her hometown of Cologne. Although Berk did not know Pilates and purportedly did not study his system of exercise (Fairfax, personal communication, 2017; Cheshire, personal communication, 2020), there may have been an indirect influence on Berk's creation of Rehabilitative Exercise. Moreover, the way that the Pilates exercise system has been used as the foundation for a contemporary dance technique draws on a rationale for making the case that Berk's methodology, which was itself informed by Berk's contemporary dance background, is highly suitable for use in the performing arts.

Throughout the history of dance, the combining of art and fitness has been documented, showing how the two complement each other and inferring that components of arts and fitness programmes are highly adaptable to applications in dance.

## Dance Education in Higher Education

In the United States, the relationship between fitness and the arts can be viewed in the history of dance studies in higher education. Sarah Hilsendager, professor of dance at Temple University Boyer College of Music and Dance, makes the association between physical education and dance education: 'Dance is unique among arts disciplines in that it is both "of" and "distinct from" its historical parent—physical education…' (Hanna, 1999, p. 56).

Margaret Newall H'Doubler, who founded the first dance programme at the University of Wisconsin, Madison, in 1926, had a scientific background in biology and was part of the physical education department (Ross, 2000). It was H'Doubler who also introduced the concept of dance education at Columbia University Teacher's College as a visiting doctoral biology student in 1916. It was H'Doubler's science-based physical education programme for dance at the University of Wisconsin, Madison, that instituted dance education in higher education in the United States (Hanna, 2006, p. 54).

The education system in the United States (K-12) has recently adopted new laws that establish arts programming (dance, music, theater, and the visual arts) as 'core subjects' based on scientific research that finds the arts beneficial to learners. These findings come from fields outside the arts, including nonverbal communications (Hinde, 1972; Wolfgang, 1984), socio and psycholinguistics (Hymes, 1974), semiotics (Sebeok, 2012), cognition (Dennett, 1991; Eisner, 1982; Gardner, 1983, 1991, 1998; Resnick, 1989), transfer of learning skills (Cormier & Hagman, 1987; Salomon & Perkins, 1989; Singley & Anderson, 1989), and in dance therapy (American Journal of Dance Therapy) (Hanna, 1999). The current trend in the United States that recognises the value of the arts in education is supported by the emergence and embrace of STEAM- (science, technology, engineering, arts, and mathematics) versus STEM-based education:

> STEAM education takes the concept of STEM education and moves it to the next
> level, incorporating the founding principles of this method with a broader artistic
> set of subjects, giving students a more holistic understanding. STEM education
> has always prioritised a practical approach to learning by encouraging students to
> question, challenge and critique within the realms of science and technology. This
> method of applied learning is extended into STEAM education, which is designed
> to grant students an even more rounded appreciation of the world. (Nord Anglia
> Education, 2020)

As noted in Chapter 2, education leaders Jonas Wright, San Francisco Conservatory of Music, and James Bundy, Yale School of Dramatic Arts, spoke of the fundamental principle of 'meeting the student on their level' and the philosophy of 'process- versus product-based learning' geared to the learners' development. These current changes in the viewpoint and understanding of arts education may also suggest an elevated position for the arts in higher education programmes in the future.

In Chapter 2, Wright and Bundy defined the role of the educator in higher education in terms of their ability to mentor learners in the development of technical skills and in preparing them for a career in the performing arts. In 2017, the researcher also interviewed Shona Morris, Lead Movement Tutor, Royal Academy of Dramatic Arts[10] (RADA), on location at the school. In conversation, Morris discussed her philosophy about the creation of impactful practises for learners seeking careers in the performing arts.

At RADA and in Canada, where Morris was formerly the head of movement at the Stratford Festival Theatre, she observed a lack of a 'certain energy in the classroom' when learners' level of physical fitness was underdeveloped. Morris also found that the increased use of computers and cell phones was affecting and limiting her students' neck and shoulder mobility. These observations served as a catalyst for inserting fitness conditioning into her teaching methodology. Morris expressed her belief that it was precisely the role of the performing arts educator to create ways that programmes can benefit learners: 'The work [practise] ultimately has to be genuine and come from the teacher's toolbox of experience' (S. Morris, 2017).

**Tailoring Dance and Fitness Training**

Research shows that dance education must insert aspects of physical fitness into performing arts training and practises to create more beneficial and holistic programmes for performing artists:

> …unless dancers are physiologically honed to the same extent as they are artistically, their physical conditioning may potentially be the limiting factor in their development. Ignoring the physiological training of today's dancers could

---

[10] The Royal Academy of Dramatic Art is considered a leading vocational conservatoire in training for theatre, television, film, and radio.

eventually hamper the development of the art form. It is the continual responsibility of dance teachers and educators to develop their knowledge and understanding of the physiological demands of dance, and be aware of the options for either integrating physical fitness training into the technique class itself or providing it through supplementation. (Irvine, Redding, & Rafferty, 2011)

Likewise, as discussed in Chapter 2, the 2011 *Dance Fitness* literature review conducted by the International Association for Dance, Medicine, and Science (IADMS) states:

In light of these studies, and with increased understanding of the artistic and athletic needs of dancers in different genres, it is no longer acceptable to train dancers without preparing them physiologically for the demands of current choreographic work .... [I]n order to achieve efficient and optimal development of dance skills, conditioning work over and above daily technique class has been recommended. (Irvine, Redding, & Rafferty, 2011)

The dance and fitness books, manuals, and syllabi referenced in this thesis provide educators with structure and content guidance that can be used to tailor classes that address specific training goals, such as core strength, flexibility, cardiovascular endurance, or increased muscle strength in the legs for dynamic balance, as required for classical ballet.

In the traditional dance academy, students are commonly placed according to age and level of proficiency, and these factors remain constant throughout their time at the school. However, in higher education, it is not uncommon for learners in the dance classroom to be of different levels, backgrounds, and from varied arts disciplines (i.e., drama, dance, opera, musical theatre, voice), and most of whom will not have had 'typical' ballet training (e.g., Royal Academy of Dance, Bournonville, Vaganova, Cecchetti). For this reason, dance education in higher education requires unique strategies that tailor programmes to 'meet the student at their level', integrating artistry with fitness conditioning.

## Barre for Performing Arts Curricula

During a 2017 interview, the researcher asked Esther Fairfax to clarify whether she considered Barre as fitness or art, and if she thought the methodology would be transferrable to a university performing arts department. Fairfax responded:

I'm sure it could. I think it would have to be very carefully viewed so it doesn't get mixed up with a lot of the sort of fitness people. It could be very interesting... I think the very fact that you want to bring the method out to the more art forms, which she wanted and said, 'I'm not a fitness person, I'm a dancer. I'm a creator.

And she was, she created a fantastic technique that is still pretty unique.' (Fairfax, 2017)

To this end, the researcher has devised a leading-edge Barre programme specifically tailored for performing arts curricula that synthesises Berk's original methodology with Bach's sports conditioning elements and Fairfax's user-friendly approach. During the course of doctoral study, the researcher has created a video-documentary and a teacher training manual, both entitled *The High Barre*, as well as an original system for documenting the pairing of movement kinematics and musical accompaniment in choreography, *The Jacobs Method of Notation*, to support The High Barre programme. *The High Barre* and *The Jacobs Method of Notation* manuals may be purchased by contacting the author at www.jillrosejacobs.com.

The High Barre's mission is to use Barre methodology to engage the learner's physical and psychological development of proprioception, individualised artistic expression, and the physical fortitude to support these pursuits.

# Chapter 4.    Case Study 1.
# Self-reported physiological and psychological effects of Barre compared with Zumba/Dance Fit

## Abstract

**Background**: Barre is presently known as a fitness format which incorporates disciplines including yoga, ballet, and Pilates. Barre methodology was developed in London in 1959 by Lotte Berk, a former contemporary dancer and classically trained pianist. Barre methodology is unique in its combination of highly repetitive isometric[11] and range-of-motion[12] exercises that target and fatigue one muscle group at a time to exhaustion, a process also known as 'specificity'. Barre programmes are characterized by sound biomechanical exercises performed in challenging sequences that normally do not travel across the floor, but whose movement is typically restricted to a limited area. In comparison, dance-fitness programmes such as Zumba and Dance Fit are characterized by choreographed, dance-movement sequences that travel around the room.

Because there are no previous academic studies on Barre to date, there are no resources from the Academy to compare in terms of benefits to learners; however, current mainstream literature about Barre claims improvement in participants' muscle strength, tone, control, body shape, posture, flexibility, and confidence in less time than other dance-fitness programmes.

**Methods/Materials**: This study included thirty-six female participants, aged between 19 and 59. A total of twenty participants were recruited from Barre classes, sixteen from Zumba/Dance Fit, and two participants from the Zumba/Dance Fit group that identified themselves as also participating in other dance-related practises. Participants were asked to complete a specifically designed questionnaire, containing twenty-six open-ended questions, which was approved by the Queen's University Ethics Committee (see Appendix E). The questionnaire asked participants about the physiological and psychological effects of the classes they took.

**Results**: Participants reported physiological (muscle strength, tone, slimming, and posture) and psychological (uplifted mood and confidence) improvements from attending Barre

---

[11] Isometric exercises are a type of strength training in which the joint angle and muscle do not change during contraction.

[12] Range of motion is how far you can move your joints in different directions.

and Zumba/Dance Fit classes. They also reported positive effects from the use of music. Those who participated in the Barre group reported marginally greater results with fewer classes compared to those who participated in the Zumba/Dance Fit group.

**Conclusion:** The study provides evidence that participants in dance-related programmes experience physiological and psychological benefits from the combination of movement and music. Moreover, while Barre participants took a fewer number of classes overall, they registered marginally greater physiological and psychological benefits than did participants in the Zumba/Dance Fit group.

## Introduction

This study examines the physiological and psychological effects of undertaking Barre, Zumba, and Dance Fit classes using a self-reporting questionnaire.

Barre comprises a full-body workout that combines exercises from yoga, ballet, and Pilates (Wahlgren, 2020; Fairfax, 2010, p. 76; Deczynski, 2016; Helmer, 2020). Its methodology is repetitive in nature and known to be physically challenging, targeting one specific anatomic muscle group at a time by alternating between isometric and range-of-motion exercises (Hughes, 2015; Seidel, 2016). Zumba is an aerobic fitness programme that combines Latin American and international music with dance movement and rhythms that alternate the beats per minute (BPM) and was developed in the 1990s by dancer and choreographer Alberto 'Beto' Perez (Laskowski, 2018; Helmer, 2020; Powell, 2016). Dance Fit is an aerobic programme that incorporates many forms of dance exercise using different rhythms and was developed in 2016 by Matthew Harrison and Andrew Buse, two British fitness instructors (Williams, 2018).

The researcher's hypothesis prior to the investigations held that dance-fitness classes produce varying degrees of improvement in muscle strength, tone/shape, mood, and confidence, and that Barre produces superior results over the course of fewer classes compared with other dance-fitness programmes.

## Methods and Materials

### *Methods*

A self-completing questionnaire (see Appendix C) was developed and distributed to thirty volunteers who were members of the Queen's University, Belfast, Physical Education

Centre (PEC), and six volunteers who were members of the Crescent Arts Centre (CAC), for a total of thirty-six volunteers.

The questionnaire was divided into three sections, each with a different objective. Each of these sections was assigned a completion date within the second term at Queen's University, Belfast, which ran from 8 January to 1 June 2018, with data collection spread evenly over a five-month period.

The three-part questionnaire asked participants to provide information as follows:

1. **Day 1** = Participants were asked to provide their personal information; prior dance/fitness/sport activity and/or hobbies; and motivation for participating in dance-fitness classes.
2. **Midterm** = Participants were asked if they were experiencing changes that could be attributed to the class, during or directly following class participation.
3. **Final Day of Term** = Participants were asked to assess whether they had achieved their goals and if others had observed any physiological changes.

The PEC offered five weekly drop-in classes: four Zumba classes and one Dance Fit class, which were available to PEC members free of charge. One weekly Barre class was also scheduled at the PEC, with another Barre course being offered through the Queen's University Staff Well-Being programme to members and non-members for a fee.

Instructors from the Barre, Zumba, and Dance Fit classes met on two occasions to discuss administering the questionnaire for completion of the study. Instructors distributed questionnaires at the beginning of their class. Participants were asked to complete a section of the questionnaire, which was then collected by the instructor, placed in labelled folders, and returned to the researcher for storage. At the end of the term, after all participants had completed their questionnaire, the researcher entered the data into Microsoft Excel for analysis, a process that revealed common themes which were then assigned a numerical value. This method provided a system for calculating final numerical scores that produced the study findings.

The participants' responses were assigned values as follows: a score of (1) was recorded for each time that the theme was reported; (n/a) meaning the participant did not answer the question; or (0) for responses that were not commonly reported but were unique to an individual's experience, which will be discussed in greater detail in the Data Analysis section.

The number of participant responses to Sections 2 and 3 declined in rate. When the researcher queried instructors about this decline, they reported that drop-in (no-fee) class attendance was inconsistent and, therefore, instructors were unfamiliar with the identity of participants, rendering it impossible to facilitate questionnaire completion as planned. All participants in the study completed Section 1 of the questionnaire; and though fewer participants completed Sections 2 and 3, all responses received were recorded and included in the research data.

*Materials*

The three-part questionnaire included a total of twenty-six open-ended questions: eight of which asked for personal information about participants' height, age, weight, hobbies, background in sports and/or dance, injuries, and motivation for attending a dance-fitness programme; ten of which inquired about participants' physiological and/or psychological experiences during and/or following their dance-fitness class; and eight of which queried participants' observations regarding their accomplishments on completion of their programme.

**Participants**

All thirty-six participants were female and aged between 19 and 59, with an average age of 33 years. Heights ranged from 157 centimetres to 175 centimetres, with an average of 164 centimetres (5'4"); and weights ranged from 53 to 122 kilograms, averaging 63.5 kilograms (140 pounds). The participants reported being healthy, with two under physician care for eye conditions, and one receiving care for asthma.

**Procedures and Data Analysis**

After full completion of questionnaires (all three sections), which coincided with the end of the university term, the data was collected and input into Microsoft Excel. The researcher consulted with a PhD candidate from the Department of Mathematics and Statistics for assistance creating the charts and graphs below. Each participant's responses were reviewed and analysed, and the information extracted and assigned a numerical value. Responses were also categorized according to each participant's enrolment in Barre or Zumba/Dance Fit.

The application for reviewing data involved the assignment of a value, as previously discussed (see **Methods**). This system produced numerical scores that gave the data meaning

(Austin & Sutton, 2015; Sibley & Etnier, 2003). The following is an example of how the information was reviewed and analysed:

**Question:** 'What do you like about your dance class?'

**Response:** 'It was "fun" and "the music made me feel good."'

The response above indicates that the class experience had a positive effect on the learner and, therefore, was assigned a value of one (1). It was also reported that the learner found the music uplifting and experienced a change of mood as a result. Therefore, another value of one (1) was assigned, because the in-class music's effect on mood was identified as a common theme among the responses. Therefore, the response to this question would have been assigned a total score of two (2).

However, if a participant provided a response that said 'it relieves my back pain,' and that response was specific to only that participant, then that response was scored with a zero (0). In the event that other participants reported back-pain relief, the data would have indicated this as a theme and the response given a value of one (1). Questions that were left blank or unanswered received a non-applicable (n/a) score of zero (0).

**Results**

During the process of data analysis, three questions were eliminated from the study as a result of participant feedback that they were either repetitive or confusing. Seven questions resulted in higher scores for participants enrolled in Barre; two questions resulted in higher values for Zumba/Dance Fit; and six of the questions were answered identically, irrespective of whether the class taken was Barre or Zumba/Dance Fit.

The data indicated that the majority of participants in the Barre group (55%) had prior dance-related experience compared to participants in the Zumba/Dance Fit group (44%). The participants most commonly reported that their motivation for enrolling in dance-fitness programmes was that they were 'fun' and/or 'low-impact'. Two participants in the Zumba/Dance Fit group identified themselves as being regular participants in either contemporary dance or Pilates classes. While the study did not find commonalities in participants' specific hobbies/activities, the findings highlighted only slight variations in participants' regular fitness routines. For example, on average Barre participants reported engaging in three to four hours of weekly exercise; whereas the average participant in Zumba/Dance Fit programmes engaged in three hours of exercise per week. The majority (99%) of total participants reported that they were making changes to their diet by 'reducing sugars', 'making healthier choices', and/or 'dieting for weight loss'.

**Figures**

The following charts and bar graphs represent participants' responses recorded from the information gathered.

**Figure 4-1 Pre-study Participation in Dance-Fitness Programmes**

Figure 4.1 illustrates that 55% of the total participants in the study were enrolled in Barre; 45% of participants were enrolled in Zumba or Dance Fit (PEC); and of the 45% Zumba/Dance Fit group, 3% identified as participating in Pilates and 3% identified as participating in contemporary dance at the time of the study.

**Figure 4-2 Participants Self-Reported Experience from Dance-Fitness Session(s) During the Study**

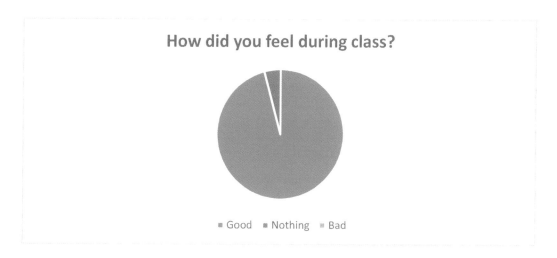

How did you feel during class?

■ Good   ■ Nothing   ■ Bad

The majority of participants (96%) reported that attending dance-movement classes produced positive effects.

**Figure 4-3 Change in Mood as a Result of Dance-Related Activity**

## Has mood, confidence or wellbeing changed?

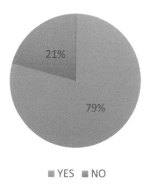

21%

79%

■ YES   ■ NO

The majority of participants (79%) reported changes in relation to mood, confidence, or well-being that resulted from dance-related activity. Responses were identical, irrespective of participation in Barre or Zumba/Dance Fit.

**Figure 4-4 Self-Reported Effects Following Dance-Related Activity**

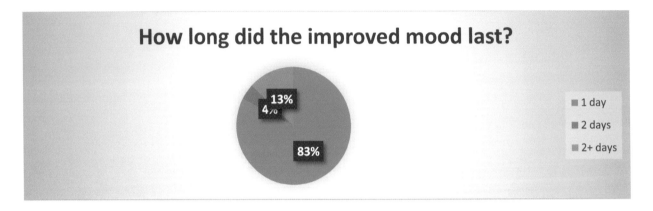

The majority of participants (87%) reported that their mood was improved following a session, and that the improvement lasted for an average of one to two days, with 13% of participants reporting that improved mood lasted until their next class.

**Figure 4-5 Achievement of Dance-Related Activity Goals**

The majority of participants (95%) reported improved muscle strength, tone, confidence, and mood as a result of their dance-related activity. The participants enrolled in the Barre group exhibited a marginally greater average score (1.8) in the positive effects of their dance-related course compared with the average score of the Zumba/Dance Fit group (1.4). Commonly, participants simply answered 'yes' to the question asked, which elicited a score value of one (1). Any additional information beyond the scope of the specific question posed but pertaining to a different study-related theme was also given a score of one (1).

**Figure 4-6 Effects of Music on Dance-Related Activity**

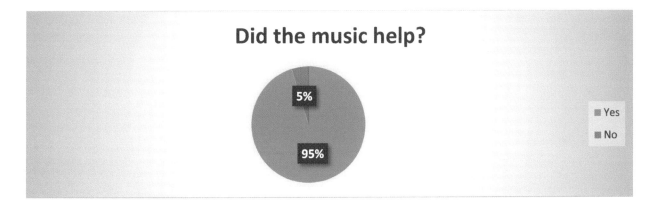

Figure 4.6 shows that 95% of participants reported that the in-class music positively contributed to their Barre and Zumba/Dance Fit experience. Three questions regarding the use of in-class music resulted in slight scoring differences, discussed below.

**Figure 4-7 Self-Reported Physiological and Psychological Improvements**

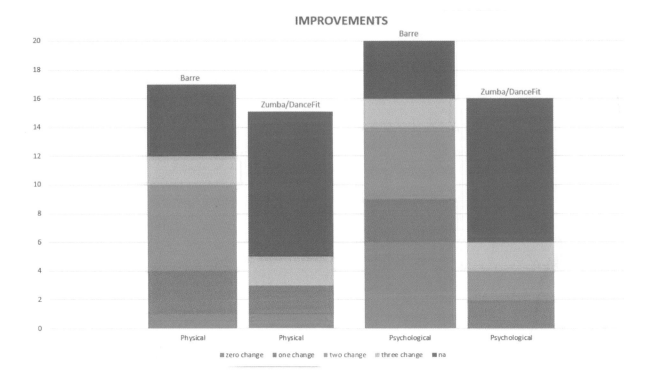

Figure 4.7 shows categorical data pertaining to physiological and psychological improvements extrapolated from participant responses to the questionnaire. The number on the left axis represents the total number of participants. The number of changes reported by participants are represented as follows:

- no (0) reported change indicated in light blue
- one (1) reported change indicated in orange
- two (2) reported changes indicated in grey
- three (3) reported changes indicated in yellow
- non-applicable (n/a) indicated in dark blue

54

Each improvement was given a value of one (1), with a maximum score of four (4). Themes included (a) muscle tone/shape, (b) flexibility, (c) confidence, and (d) mood.

**Figure 4-8 What Could be Better (i.e., the Exercises, Movements, or Music) and Why?**

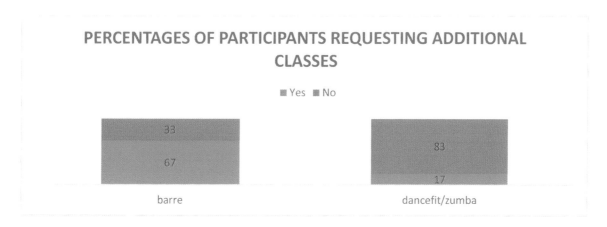

The questionnaire asked participants, 'What could be better (i.e., the exercises, movements, or music) and why?' Interestingly, the majority of Barre participants (67%) commented that an increase in the number of Barre classes given would be 'better', even though they were not expressly asked or prompted to do so. However, only 17% of the Zumba/Dance Fit participants thought that more classes would be beneficial. Perhaps this was because more of the Zumba/Dance Fit classes were already being offered. The result may also suggest that Barre participants experienced a sense of achievement that they expected would increase with more opportunities to practise.

**Figure 4-9 Are the Exercises Getting Easier to Do, Harder, or No Different?**

The majority of Barre participants (87.5%) reported that the exercises became easier as the term progressed 'until the routine/choreography changed'. Meanwhile, the majority of the Zumba/Dance Fit participants (67%) reported that the routines became easier, but had no further comment(s). This difference may be the result of Barre's repetitious strength-conditioning practises as opposed to Zumba/Dance Fit routines that are largely cardiovascular driven. Whereas Zumba/Dance Fit routines develop stamina, which does not decrease when routines change, the Barre practise of specificity renews the challenge each time different muscle groups are targeted.

**Figure 4-10 Have Other People Commented on Changes in You, and if so, What Have They Said?**

Figure 4.10 illustrates the participants' responses to the question, 'Have other people commented on changes in you, and if so, what have they said?' Barre participants (87%) and

Zumba/Dance Fit participants (83%) reported that comments were made by others about their increased muscle strength, tone, and/or slimmer appearance.

**Discussion**

Questionnaire results show that combined participant scores varied only marginally in categorical comparison. Figure 4.2 highlights that the majority of participants (96%) described their respective classes as 'uplifting', 'energising', 'challenging', or made other positive comments, with one respondent even noting, 'I feel like a dancer'. Figure 4.3 illustrates similar scores among participants in the Barre and Zumba/Dance Fit groups pertaining to improved mood, confidence, and/or well-being.

Empirical investigations on cognition have found a link between improvements in physiological and psychological well-being and dance movement (Rehfeld, et al., 2017, 2018; Hamacher et al., 2015; Kattenstroth et al., 2010; Edwards, 2015). The Harvard Mahoney Neuroscience Institute's article 'Dancing and the Brain' reports:

> … fitness and dance have previously been shown to be associated with other beneficial effects including increased aerobic capacity, improved body composition, greater bone density, muscular size and strength, improved psychological well-being, increased self-esteem and reduced anxiety. (Edwards, 2015)

Evidence indicates that dance programmes can have prolonged, far-reaching, and positive effects (Duberg et al., 2013). Figure 4.4 shows that the majority of participants (87%) reported psychological improvements following their class sessions that lasted for one to two days, with the remaining 13% saying that improvements continued 'until the next class'. However, there was no specific question that asked participants to quantify the exact duration of improvement.

In response to the question: 'Did you achieve your goals?', shown in Figure 4.5, participants most commonly responded, 'yes', an answer that was assigned a score of one (1). Reframing this question in a multiple-choice format may have produced more specific data, which will be discussed below in the **Limitations** section.

Shown in Figure 4.6, participants highlighted the positive effects produced by musical accompaniment, reporting that 'it made the exercises easier' and 'more enjoyable'. No information was collected on the genre or type of music used during participants' dance-related classes. The music used for all practices (Barre, Zumba, and Dance Fit) was selected by instructors to enhance learners' in-class experience. An article in *American Scientist* magazine quotes Columbia University neuroscientist Daniel Tarsy, MD, who posits the relationship between music and movement as being a 'pleasure double play' in the way that music stimulates the brain's reward centres, while dance activates its sensory and motor circuits (Edwards, 2015). An experienced instructor can combine music to movement kinematics to systematically frame and give structure to the lesson plan, a process that also provides cognitive benefits. The relationship between music and movement and its links to cognition will be explored in Chapter 5.

Participants were also asked: 'Did the music have any (positive or negative) effect on the challenging exercise sequences?' The majority of Barre participants (93%) and all of the Zumba/Dance Fit participants reported that the music made performing the exercises easier and made the class more pleasurable. This finding may be a result of Barre's greater technical demands versus those of Zumba/Dance Fit, or it may be attributed to the higher BPM used in more cardiovascular-driven training programmes, like Zumba and Dance Fit. Research suggests that upbeat tempos of 135 BPM and higher have physiologically elevating effects whose durations are short-lived (Karageorghis & Terry, 2011; Landoli, 2017; Madden, 2014).

Barre classes in this study paired movement kinematics to music whose BPM ranged between 90 and 130. Barre participants in this study reported a marginal difference in psychological improvement (one to two days) compared with Zumba/Dance Fit participants (one day). This suggests that instructors of Barre, Zumba, and Dance Fit, among others, would do well to understand and embrace the importance of combining movement and music in the classroom in a way that produces more impactful benefits for learners.

In Figure 4.7, the participants recorded improvements in 'muscle strength', 'tone', 'confidence', and 'mood'. The results showed a marginal categorical variance reported by Barre participants (mean value of 1.8) versus Zumba/Dance Fit participants (mean value of 1.4).

Figures 4.7, 4.8, 4.9, and 4.10 illustrate the categorical variables for participants in Barre and Zumba/Dance Fit classes using stacked bar graphs. The questions corresponding to these graphs were in Section 2 of the questionnaire, a section whose rate of responses began declining, as noted earlier in this study (see **Methods**).

Overall, the findings in this study suggest that participation in Barre and Zumba/Dance Fit classes have positive physiological and psychological effects on learners. It is important to note that the Zumba/Dance Fit participants had an advantage over Barre participants in terms of practice frequency, with a ratio being three (3) weekly Barre classes to five (5) weekly Zumba and Dance Fit classes. This notwithstanding, the study shows that the Barre group experienced benefits that were similar to the Zumba/Dance Fit group, even though the Barre group participated in fewer practise sessions. Had there been an even distribution of practises among the groups, greater categorical variations may have been notable.

**Limitations**

Discussion of the data takes into consideration a non-sampling error that resulted from the participants' partial completion of Sections 2 and 3 of the questionnaires. Valuations were made based on the data collected and from the questions answered. The average percentage of participants that failed to complete the questionnaire from the Zumba/Dance Fit group was 35% compared with the Barre group average of 17%. This may suggest that participants registered for and attended classes more regularly when they paid a fee than when they attended drop-in classes, which were free to members of the PEC.

Additionally, the use of multiple-choice questionnaires would have elicited more detailed responses from which to draw conclusions—information that could be used to create more impactful programmes. Moreover, it would have been more efficient to employ a data collection method that could be completed and submitted within the class session. Despite the limitations of this study, it represents the first to investigate Barre in the academic arena.

# Chapter 5.     Case Study 2
# A comparison of Barre and Zumba/Dance Fit on standing leg stability and the physiological and psychological impact of musical accompaniment on overall movement quality

## Background

Case Study 1 in Chapter 4 provided evidence of improvement in muscle strength, tone, and control; confidence; and mood among Barre and Zumba/Dance Fit participants. Furthermore, the majority of participants reported that music had played a positive role in their enjoyment of the classes. These findings are supported by existing dance and fitness research that investigate the effects on cognition when pairing movement to music in choreography (Duberg et al., 2013; Rehfeld et al., 2017, 2018; Muller et al., 2017; Stonnington et al., 2019).

Case Study 2, presented in this chapter, further investigates the physiological and psychological effects of Barre versus Zumba/Dance Fit using resources on location in the Movement Innovation Lab (MIL) at Queen's University, Belfast.

## Case Study 2

This two-part study investigates the following:

1. the physiological impact on standing leg stability (muscle strength and control) of Barre versus Zumba/Dance Fit practises
2. the physiological and psychological impact of musical accompaniment versus scripted verbal instructions on overall movement quality when performing a choreographed movement sequence

## Experiment Protocol

**Participants**: In this study, participants (n = 24) were healthy adult women (n = 23) and/or men (n = 1), ages 19 to 53, with a mean of 33 years. Fifteen volunteers were enrolled in Barre classes (n = 15), and 9 volunteers were enrolled in Zumba/Dance Fit (n = 9). These programmes were offered through the Physical Education Centre (PEC) at Queen's University, Belfast (QUB), or Crescent Arts Centre (CAC), located on the university campus. The Movement Innovation Lab (MIL), where this case study was conducted, is located in the PEC. Participants were individually tested in two phases:

- Phase 1: 18 March – 20 April 2018
- Phase 2: 17 May – 2 June 2018

The researcher/expert administered the dynamic balance test to the participants in this study, demonstrating the Barre sequences using verbal instruction. The researcher/expert is experienced teaching dance and sports fitness internationally, performed professionally in ballet and musical theatre companies, and was a professor in the performing arts department at New York University. The researcher/expert has also instructed Barre programmes for the Equinox and other corporate fitness companies in the United States and the United Kingdom.

## Study Design, Preparations, and Apparatus

**Figure 5-1 Jill Rose Jacobs Dance Study**

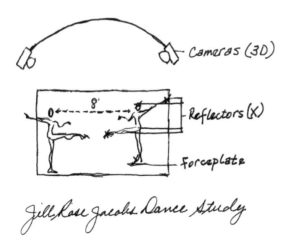

**Figure 5-2 Researcher/Expert and Participant in Position in the Movement Innovation Lab (MIL)**

The MIL was pre-set with an area to accommodate the traveling movement used in Zumba and Dance Fit and an area for performing the Barre sequence exercise, using adjustable support frames in place of barres (apparatus). The Barre sequence exercise was recorded by the Qualisys 3D motion capture system running at 500Hz and an AMTI portable Accugait force platform. Reflective markers were used to collect data on muscle control, posture, movement patterns, trajectory of the limbs, and rotation of the head,[13] while the force platform collected measurements of participants' foot/ankle action and sway (see Figure 5.2). The duration of the choreographed Barre sequence exercise was 3 minutes 15 seconds, divided into three sections, and performed on the right and left supporting limb. Each side was performed once with musical accompaniment and once to a verbal script (no music). The final section of the Barre Sequence exercise, 'High-Lower-Lower-Lower' (18 seconds), was selected for analysis as the dynamic balance test.

**Procedure**

On the first visit to the MIL, participants followed this procedure:

- signed a consent form (see Appendix D).
- reflective markers were placed on middle fingers (digitus medius), big toes (hallus), and on the right and left hip (greater trochanter), and a visor with markers was placed on the head (see Figure 5.3)
- participants performed a Zumba warm-up to prepare for the choreographed Barre sequence exercise and to familiarise themselves with the researcher/expert's cueing style
- participants performed the Barre sequence exercise

When volunteering for the study, participants were informed that they would be recorded performing dance movement, but no specific information about the test or equipment had been given.

---

[13] Positioning of reflective markers was determined using guidance from the Disney Research project led by Devin Coldewey in 2016 (Coldewey, 2016).

**Figure 5-3 Reflective Markers on the Participant**

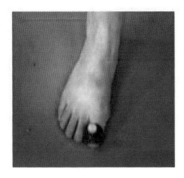 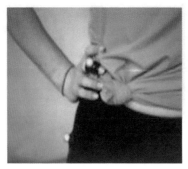 

**Test procedure:** The researcher/expert demonstrated the Barre sequence exercise with verbal instructions while the participant observed and practised in tandem. The researcher/expert then asked if the participant understood the exercise. When the researcher/expert received a verbal 'yes' or nod in confirmation, she cued the technical assistant, 'Let's begin in 4, 3, 2, 1 . . .' to start the motion capture and force platform system's recording. The participants performed the Barre sequence exercise twice, once on each supporting limb, to both sound conditions — musical accompaniment and verbal-only cues (no music).

## Sounds and Design

As noted above, the participants performed the Barre sequence exercise using two different sound conditions: (1) musical accompaniment and (2) scripted verbal-only cues (no music). In the test administered to musical accompaniment, 'Make Me Feel' by Janelle Monae was used. The song played at a rate of 115 BPM for a duration of 3 minutes 15 seconds. The verbal instructions given in both sound conditions—without music and with musical accompaniment—consisted of standard dance and fitness cues that were scripted and memorized by the researcher/expert in order to ensure consistency during the dynamic balance tests in both environments.

In the test administered without music, the researcher/expert used an earpiece which allowed her to hear the music, while the participant was only able to hear the verbal cues. This method enabled the researcher/expert to match the tempo, dynamic, and inflection of her voice in both sound environments (i.e., with music and without).

The Barre sequence exercise began with the researcher/expert demonstrating while the participant marked the exercise in tandem. Following the demonstration, the researcher/expert asked, 'Do you understand the exercise?' to which participants verbally responded or nodded 'yes'. The participant then randomly chose to begin the test with their right or left foot centred on the force platform, while the researcher/expert randomly selected the sound condition: musical accompaniment or verbal-only cues (no music).

The participant initiated the test standing on the foot closest to the support frame (standing foot) in the centre of the force platform, and the opposing foot (moving foot) extended to the front of the body, making contact with the floor. In the Barre sequence exercise 'High, Lower, Lower, Lower', the participant was asked to raise the moving limb to 90 degrees or to their maximum extension. Then they were asked to lower the moving limb downward, in one-second intervals, until the moving foot touched the floor (see Figure 5.2). Participants then turned to the other side, stood on the other foot, and performed the test to the opposing sound condition.

For the second visit to the MIL, the standing foot and the sound condition were pre-assigned by the researcher/expert in the reverse order from the participant's first test, thereby ensuring that both limbs and sound conditions were tested equally.

## Analysis

Six experts in the field of dance and fitness from the United States (New York City and Washington, D.C.); the Republic of Ireland; and Edinburgh, Scotland, collaborated on the analysis for this study. The expert evaluators (heretofore 'evaluators') were selected based on their unique knowledge and expertise.

### *Sarita Allen*

Sarita Allen, Ailey Extension faculty and founder of the Ailey Barre program, also serves as the artistic advisor for Complexions Contemporary Ballet and is a consultant and member of the HBO Wellness Team. Allen was an original member of the Alvin Ailey Repertory Ensemble and during her tenure with the Alvin Ailey American Dance Theatre, Mr. Ailey created leading roles for her which she performed at The Paris Opera, the Acropolis, the Pyramids of Giza, The Kennedy Center, and at the White House for two presidents.

### Elisabeth Halfpapp and Fred DeVito

Elisabeth Halfpapp and Fred DeVito are the founders of CoreBarreFit and authors of *Barre Fitness*, formerly founders and senior teachers at the corporate fitness franchise 'exhale' (2002–2020). As vice president and director of the original Lotte Berk Method studio in New York City (1980–2002), the couple was integral in launching Barre in the United States. Halfpapp holds an Associate Degree in Dance Education and has danced professionally with the Hartford Ballet. DeVito received a Bachelor of Science in Physical Education and Health from The College of New Jersey, and was the first male Barre instructor in the United States.

### Dr Alan Cummins

Dr Alan Cummins is a postdoctoral research fellow at Trinity University, Dublin, and directed the MIL at Queen's University, Belfast, for eight years. Cummins specializes in software development, user interface and graphic design, and creating virtual environments for sport and rehabilitation-based applications. He holds degrees in Computer Science and Psychology, a Masters in Computer Graphics, and a PhD in the use of serious games for mental health improvement.

### Kedzie Penfield

Kedzie Penfield has worked as a Laban Movement Analyst (LMA) for the last 40 years. Originally trained as a dancer and dance therapist, she uses LMA diagnostically, choreographically, and in Movement Pattern Analysis in business and team building with Warren Lamb Associates.[14] Penfield has collaborated on various research projects, including analysing body movements of musicians, actors, politicians, and psychiatric patients. She now has a psychoanalysis practise in Edinburgh.

### Peggy Hackney

Peggy Hackney is internationally known for her work in Laban/Bartneieff Movement Analysis. She performed across the United States with the Bill Evans Dance Company, among others, and has participated in many research projects that address dance style analysis, personal

---

[14] **Warren Lamb** (28 April 1923 – 21 January 2014) was a British management consultant and pioneer in the field of nonverbal behaviour. Lamb developed <u>Movement Pattern Analysis,</u> a system for analysing and interpreting movement behaviour based on the work of Rudolf Laban that has applications in the fields of management consulting, executive recruitment and therapy. Lamb used the MPA system in advising multinational corporations and government organizations at top team level.

style analysis, and motion capture work with the Green Dot project in New York City. Hackney has recently retired from teaching at the University of California – Berkley, and now gives professional movement/dance-related seminars around the world.

**Results**

Each of the evaluators was introduced to the study by viewing the 8 minute 47 second 'Jill Rose Jacobs Dance Study' video documentary produced by Queen's University, Belfast, film student Aimee Buckley (attached to thesis). The documentary records a participant in the lab following the experiment procedure outlined above. The evaluators viewed the documentary; however, they were given no other information about the study.

The evaluators were then shown graphical renderings of each participant's sequence test as recorded by 3D motion capture and force platform. Each participant's test was separated into frontal and profile images on a split screen as seen below.

**Figure 5-4 Graphical Rendering in Qualisys Track Manager**

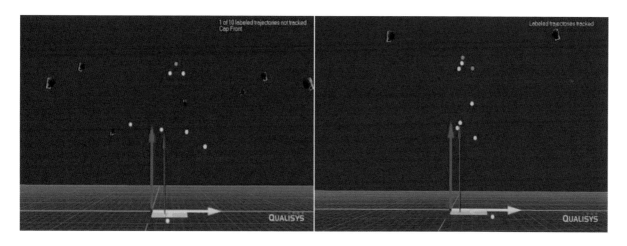

These 'dancing dots' images, a description coined by the evaluators, showed each participant's performance of the Barre sequence exercise section 'High-Lower-Lower-Lower' in 4 repetitions that lasted 18 seconds total. Participant names did not appear on the screen, nor were the evaluators informed that each participant would be viewed twice: (a) performing the sequence to musical accompaniment, and (b) performing the exercise without music to verbal-only cues. There were 48 tests in total. The evaluators viewed the participant recordings without sound, to minimise distraction during visual analysis.

**Evaluations**

After viewing the video documentary, evaluators Allen, Halfpapp, and DeVito then viewed the system's rendering of the researcher/expert performing the 18-second dynamic balance test 'High, Lower, Lower, Lower' until they were confident that they understood the data.

The evaluators were then asked to score the participants' performance of the following four technical skills on a Likert rating scale of 1 through 7 (1 = poor to 7 = excellent):

- Strength in the supporting leg/foot
- Consistency/control in the moving leg/foot
- Coordination between hand, leg, and head movements
- Posture, including core engagement

The evaluators then assessed the 24 participants performing the test using both sound conditions, completing their evaluation process.

After viewing the 3D motion capture renderings (dancing dots), evaluators Penfield and Hackney contended that a different evaluative approach would be required from them because Laban Movement Analysis (LMA) was based on the principles of 'describing, interpreting, and documenting all varieties of *human movement*', elements that were missing from the motion capture data output. In other words, their work was based on observing 'humans', and since the motion capture renderings presented only dancing dots, they suggested that their evaluative contribution would be better informed by an analysis of the MIL video documentary, through which they could observe the human form and visage of the test participant.

**Findings**

While the dance and sports evaluators assigned similar scores to both Barre and Zumba/Dance Fit groups for the dynamic balance test, the Barre group's total scores were marginally higher. The force platform data also showed similar results between the groups, with a modest indication that the Barre group participants were developing better one-legged balance skills than the Zumba/Dance Fit group.

Based on an assessment of the motion capture dancing dots, the dance and sports evaluators found that the participants performed the dynamic balance tests similarly, regardless of the sound conditions. However, based on the video documentary, the LMA evaluators disagreed regarding the impact of the sound conditions, stating that they observed physiological and psychological improvement when the participant's performance was accompanied by music rather than verbal-only cues.

## Dance and Sports Evaluator Scoring Graphs

The findings in this section are based on the dance and sports evaluators' scoring of the participants' performances based on the 3D motion capture renderings (dancing dots). The graphs and charts illustrate results of the 48 dynamic balance tests (24 participants x 2 sound conditions = 48). Groups are divided by practise type = Barre and Zumba/Dance Fit; and by sound condition = Music (musical accompaniment) or Word (verbal-only cues). The Participants Average Scores were tabulated to produce a total score, then divided by the number of participants in the group: Barre (15) and Zumba/Dance Fit (9).

**Figure 5-5 Evaluator Sarita Allen**

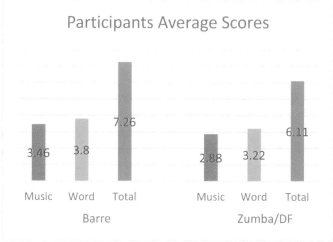

**Figure 5-6 Evaluator Elisabeth Halfpapp**

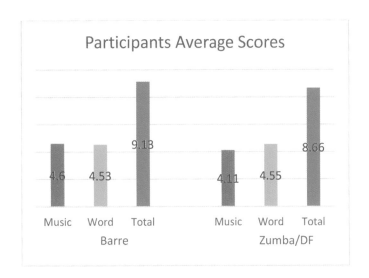

**Figure 5-7 Evaluator Fred DeVito**

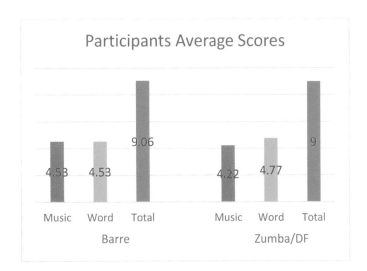

The Barre group scored marginally higher values on the performance of technical skills although the graphs indicate an overall similarity among the participants of the Barre and Zumba/Dance Fit groups. A comparative analysis of the two sound conditions produced similar findings, although there is some indication that the Zumba/Dance Fit group performed better in tests where participants were given verbal-only cues.

In the graph below, total scores were combined and are shown for each evaluator and group.

**Figure 5-8 Combined Scores from Allen, Halfpapp, and DeVito**

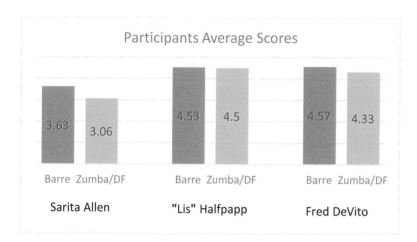

In the above graph, participant scores are similar; however, there is a suggestion that the Barre group performed modestly better than the participants of the Zumba/Dance Fit group.

## Force Platform Data

When evaluating the force platform measurements, systems analysis expert Dr Alan Cummins identified marginal differences between the groups. He found that the Barre group was developing more advanced skills in the one-legged stance, noting a trend in the foot/ankle action of the Barre group that mimicked the researcher/expert's force platform measurements (Figure 5.9).

In the Figure 5.9 graph below, Centre-of-Pressure (CoP) refers to the force platform's recording of foot/ankle motions and actions. The CoP is measured in 'sway' that is affected much in the same way as a bathroom scale is sensitive to shifting weight on its surface. This sway is calculated by the force platform movement in both lateral (from the big toe across the whole foot) and forward and back directions (from heel to toe).

When the researcher/expert performed the dynamic balance test 'High, Lower, Lower, Lower', her recorded foot/ankle action demonstrated frequent minute adjustments. This data was then compared to that of the participants:

**Figure 5-9 Centre of Pressure (CoP) Force Platform Data**

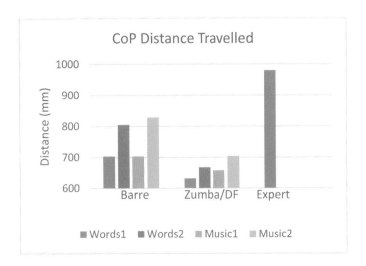

*Phase 1 tests:* Words 1 (no music, verbal-only cues), Music 1 (musical accompaniment)

*Phase 2 tests:* Words 2 (no music, verbal-only cues), Music 2 (musical accompaniment)

The graph exhibits the researcher/expert's standing foot/ankle actions compared to those of the Barre and Zumba/Dance Fit group through Phase 1 and Phase 2 testing. Interestingly, the Phase 2 results seem to indicate a trend wherein the supporting foot/ankle actions recorded for both groups begin to mimic those of the researcher/expert as the testing progresses.

**Laban Movement Analysis (LMA) Results**

As mentioned earlier, LMA evaluators Penfield and Hackney based their findings on the MIL video documentary that demonstrated a participant's performance of the dynamic balance test 'High, Lower, Lower, Lower'. They submitted collaborative evaluations as well as independent observations, identifying themselves as 'Observer A' and 'Observer B', rather than by name (see Appendix G).

In their collaborative statement, the LMA evaluators state:

We have taken 'expressivity' as a core concept to support the hypothesis that musical accompaniment has enabled a more alive, human engagement with this exercise [sequence]. Robots and machines are not expressive . . . Here, using LMA, 'human being-ness' is defined as expressivity, which in turn is identified through observable, notated qualities of movement which the subject's movement has when performed by her. (Appendix E)

The LMA evaluators are referring to the 'individual's movement signature' and how her movement quality can be observed in the MIL video documentary when she performs the dynamic balance test to musical accompaniment compared to verbal-only cues.

Penfield's and Hackney's individual evaluations summarize their findings:

**Observer A:** Here [with music] we see the whole body involved in the movement phrase rather than just an arm moving on the torso . . . Simultaneously, the head tilts forward to one side then the other; moving with an independent but integrated bobbing motion. Many more body parts are involved in an organized, flowing, and three-dimensional sequence . . . The phrasing style and the efforts used are similar to those of the first sequence [verbal-only script] but the intensity is greater and the sense of the body moving as an orchestrated 'whole' gives the viewer a sense of seeing someone who is engaged with the movement and enjoying themselves rather than trying to follow the instructor and 'get it right'. . . Her torso has a shape flow quality that adds to an impression of enjoyment and 'aliveness' to this series that was absent in the earlier filmed sequences [no music, verbal-only dialog].

**Observer B:** There are more body parts moving ... in an integrated, phrased way: the head is like an involved commentary at the beginning and into each phrase. We are watching a pleasant conversation between different body parts in the second excerpt [with music]. In the first [no music, verbal-only cues] we are watching a student attempting to 'follow the teacher' and 'get it right', which results in a more mechanical, less human and individual expression of herself.

The LMA evaluators found that the participant in the video documentary performed more consistently and with better muscle control and coordination in the choreographed Barre sequence exercise when it was paired with musical accompaniment as opposed to the verbal-only script. Moreover, they found physiological and psychological improvement in the participant's movement quality, mood, and expression when the sequence she was performing was accompanied by music.

## Discussion

The investigations in this study elicited different feedback from the dance and sports evaluators versus the LMA evaluators, which is not uncommon in dance and sports research. Referring back to the example noted in Chapter 2, multiple studies found that a once-weekly fitness intervention that increased leg-press strength in women was no more effective when performed twice weekly (Burt et al., 2007; DiFrancisco-Donoghue & Werner, 2006), while other studies asserted that greater frequency produced greater results (Ralston et al., 2018; Evans, 2019; Schoenfeld et al., 2016).

In Case Study 2, three dance and sports evaluators found that although test participants exhibited similar levels of technical skill regardless of participation in Barre or Zumba/Dance Fit, the Barre group performed slightly better based on the 3D motion capture renderings. It is notable that the Barre group in this study were novices, as Barre had only recently been introduced in Belfast, whereas those participating in the Zumba/Dance Fit group had been studying for many years prior and were practising more times per week. This may suggest that the Barre group's better score may have been even higher had its participants been given the same number of classes as the Zumba/Dance Fit group.

The systems analysis expert found that the data indicated that all participants in the study performed the dynamic balance test with similar results. However, the Barre group's CoP measurements showed the development toward more advanced balance skills and stability on the supporting foot/ankle, 'mimicking' the expert's CoP result when performing the dynamic balance test (Figure 5.9).

**Conclusion**

In this study, participants from Barre, Zumba, and Dance Fit performed a one-legged dynamic balance test to two sound conditions: (1) paired to musical accompaniment, and (2) to verbal-only cues (no music). The dynamic balance test was administered in the MIL at Queen's University, Belfast, using 3D motion capture and force platform systems. The renderings from the motion capture and force platform data were given to three dance and sports evaluators for analysis and scoring, based on each participant's performance of technical skills. While these evaluators gave the Barre and Zumba/Dance Fit groups similar scores, they rated the Barre group marginally higher. Moreover, the evaluators found no significant difference in the participants' performance, whether testing to musical accompaniment or verbal-only cues.

In contrast, two LMA evaluators found that a video documentary of a participant's performance of the choreographed Barre sequence exercise, which included the dynamic balance test 'High, Lower, Lower, Lower', showed positive physiological and psychological effects when the Barre sequence exercise was performed to musical accompaniment versus verbal-only cues. The LMA evaluators cited improvement in the participant's movement quality, muscle control and coordination, mood, and expression when the choreographed Barre sequence exercise was paired to musical accompaniment.

**Limitations**

The dance and sports evaluators scored the participants in the study based on their particular area of expertise and experience. The technical skill guidelines, such as 'coordination between hand, leg, and head movements', would have had a different meaning to the evaluator trained in ballet (where the eye follows the middle finger) than the evaluator with a background in sports. The 3D motion capture renderings, referred to by the dance and sports evaluators as 'dancing dots', may have also proved difficult to understand in rating participants' performances. Also, the act of watching the researcher/expert as she performed the exercise along with them would have limited the participants' use of head/hand coordination as they too performed the exercise.

The LMA evaluators who viewed a video documentary of a participant performing the dynamic balance tests in the MIL had a very different interpretation than the dance and sports evaluators. According to the LMA evaluators, the study showed the positive effects of performing the choreographed Barre sequence exercise to musical accompaniment. The difference in these evaluators' findings may suggest that the video documentary was a better method for analysis than the systems renderings and/or that LMA is a preferred analytic method for this type of research.

To prepare for this study, the researcher/expert compiled studies on motion capture systems and reviewed research about how to place reflective markers on the body for best results (Coldewey, 2016). In hindsight, additional markers on the ankles, knees, shoulders, and elbows would have generated a fuller human-like form than the 'dancing dots' image. The Qualisys 3D motion capture system has the capacity to render a human-like figure that may have further assisted evaluator analysis and contributed more data to the study—in other words, more markers would have equalled more data.

The researcher/expert drew inspiration for this study based on one-legged dynamic balance research (Watson et al., 2017; Alderton, Moritz, & Moe-Nilssen, 2003; Rasool & George, 2007; McLeod et al., 2009; Lin et al., 2014; Hopper, Weidemann, & Karin, 2018) and on cognition studies that examine the effects on the brain of dance compared to fitness interventions (Rehfeld et al., 2017, 2018; Muller et al., 2017; Hamacher et al., 2015; Kattenstroth et al., 2010; Stonnington et al., 2019). Recent studies highlight the benefits of pairing musical accompaniment with choreographed movement compared to unchoreographed fitness conditioning when music is only used for atmospheric and motivational purposes. For example, **'Dancing or Fitness Sport? The Effects of Two Training Programs on Hippocampal Plasticity and Balance Abilities in Healthy Seniors',** speaks to the effects of participation in dance interventions as having the potential to 'reverse the signs of aging on the brain' (Rehfeld et al., 2017). Another study, 'Dance training is superior to repetitive physical exercise in inducing brain plasticity in the elderly', illustrates the greater benefits of dance versus fitness conditioning, as shown in the graph below:

**Figure 5-10 Individual Changes in Plasma BDNF [brain-derived neurotrophic factor] Level after Intervention**

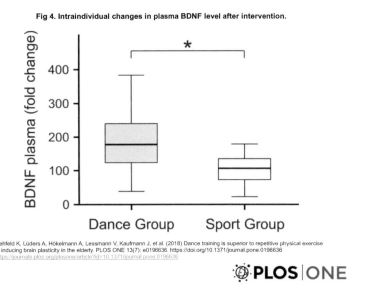

Fig 4. Intraindividual changes in plasma BDNF level after intervention.

Rehfeld K, Lüders A, Hökelmann A, Lessmann V, Kaufmann J, et al. (2018) Dance training is superior to repetitive physical exercise in inducing brain plasticity in the elderly. PLOS ONE 13(7): e0196636. https://doi.org/10.1371/journal.pone.0196636
https://journals.plos.org/plosone/article?id=10.1371/journal.pone.0196636

**PLOS | ONE**

The findings show that participation in both dance and sports increases the flow of blood in the brain; however, the data reveals a significant increase in blood flow to the brain in the group that practised dance. According to Dr Matthew Rodger, professor of psychology at Queen's University, Belfast, 'there is evidence that the change in blood flow in the brain that occurs with choreographed exercises, like dance, in comparison to non-choreographed physical activity, can increase up to four times … when comparing those two groups' (Rodger, personal communication, *The High Barre,* 2020).

Zumba has been recently examined in studies on cognition. One such study, 'Impact of Zumba on Cognition and Quality of Life is Independent of APOE4 Carrier Status in Cognitively Unimpaired Older Women: A 6-Month Randomized Controlled Pilot Study', found that participation in Zumba practises improved specific brain functions:

> We observed that repeated practice of learning and inhibiting dance moves may have strengthened performance on visuospatial working memory and response tasks in the Zumba as compared to the control group . . . (Stonnington et al., 2019)

A literature review of thirteen studies, which included 1605 participants, concluded that 'dance may be a safe and effective approach to improve cognitive function in older adults' (Meng et al., 2019, p. 17).

While the studies on cognition are beyond the scope of this thesis, further investigation of the efficacity of choreographed Barre sequence interventions paired with musical accompaniment may be considered for research, particularly in studies with older women (> 60 years old), as the format is popular with this demographic. Lotte Berk taught until she was 80 years old and practised until she was 85. Esther Fairfax taught and practised until the age of 88, and Lydia Bach continues to teach and practise in her early 80s.

# Chapter 6.    Conclusion

**Does Barre methodology's fitness/arts approach present a uniquely modernised, dance-based foundation that can benefit learners in higher education performing arts programmes?**

This thesis queries the potential for Barre methodology as dance education in higher education performing arts curricula. The data records new information about Barre through ethnographic interviews, critical analysis of the existing literature and media sources, and two case studies. In conclusion, this thesis offers a means by which to understand the origins and evolution of Barre and how the methodology can be tailored to benefit learners in higher education performing arts curricula.

**What is Barre and how has it evolved?**

Chapter 1 presents data from the literature, media sources, and ethnographic interviews to understand the origins and history of Barre. Different accounts surfaced about the innovator, Lotte Berk, and her original dance-based programme, compelling the researcher to employ a triangulated approach to validate the veracity of the information.

The current literature and media sources portray Berk as a highly sexualized and eccentric character whose classes attracted a celebrity clientele, a focus that overshadows Berk's actual innovation and information about the structure and content of her original programme. In addition, the literature and media sources were found to give inaccurate accounts of Berk's history, background, and the stimulus that motivated Berk to create her programme.

Berk's daughter, Esther Fairfax, provided testimony to fill in gaps in the historical information found in the current literature and media sources. Fairfax's interview was video-recorded in her home in Hungerford, Berkshires, in 2017, and the documentary *An Interview with Esther Fairfax* is attached to this thesis. Notably, the video-documentary evidences that the backstory of Berk's innovation, often recorded as motivated by self-rehabilitation for injuries suffered in a car accident that left Berk confined to a wheelchair, are 'in fact?—fake!' according to Fairfax. She states that her mother needed a means of financial support following a romantic break-up that left her with a morphine addiction from which she also needed to recover. Moreover, the documentary records information leading directly into the creation of

Rehabilitative Exercise, the name Berk gave to her original programme, that is not found in the media sources.

In conversations with Berk's former students and teacher trainees, including Berk's thirty-five-year licensee, Lydia Bach, it was revealed that Berk and Fairfax had been estranged for nearly three decades. This finding explains some of the inaccuracies in the media that often refers to Fairfax as the expert on Berk and her programme. Moreover, because Fairfax did not have a performing arts background, as did her mother, Fairfax's translation of her mother's programme did not convey important aspects of its dance underpinning.

In summary, Chapter 1 traces the evolution of Berk's original dance-based programme, Rehabilitative Exercise, and how it informed the development of two other fitness programmes that became prevalent in the United Kingdom and the United States, respectively: Fairfax's user-friendly exercise system, the Lotte Berk Technique; and Bach's sports-based programme, the Lotte Berk Method.

## How is Barre currently being used and what are potential future applications?

The Chapter 2 investigations are two-part. The first section examines current Barre programmes, the structure and content of Barre practises, and the way that Barre practise effects participants, based on testimonials. In addition, the first section examines the research on dance and the efficacy of traditional dance methods for training in the performing arts. The study 'Dance Fitness', published by the International Association for Dance Medicine and Science, encapsulates the findings of the current dance research:

> ...unless dancers are physiologically honed to the same extent as they are artistically, their physical conditioning may potentially be the limiting factor in their development. Ignoring the physiological training of today's dancers could eventually hamper the development of the art form. It is the continual responsibility of dance teachers and educators to develop their knowledge and understanding of the physiological demands of dance, and be aware of the options for either integrating physical fitness training into the technique class itself or providing it through supplementation. (Irvine, Redding, & Rafferty, 2011)

The second section explores the potential applications for Barre methodology beyond its place in fitness. A generous award to the researcher on behalf of ICURe (Innovation to Commercialisation of University Research) funded global travel to conduct interviews with leaders in the fields of medicine, media, education, the performing arts, and health and wellness industries to gain insights into using Barre as a problem-solving methodology to address deficiencies within their respective areas of expertise.

The data collected in the meetings produced seven common areas of concern among the interviewees: 1) physical and mental injury; 2) weight issues; 3) lack of movement opportunities; 4) education of teachers; 5) process- versus product-based learning; 6) career transitions for retiring professional performing artists; and 7) programmes for injury prevention. Each of these areas was then researched and critically analysed. In relationship to the performing arts, the investigations found a high rate of physical and mental injury among performing artists caused by poor physical conditioning, stress, substance abuse, stage conditions, ill-fitting costumes, among other issues. The interviewees also revealed a stark assessment of the health complications caused by often stringent efforts to attain the desired classical ballet aesthetic that requires an ultra-thin body type and use of 180-degree turn-out, both touchstones for professional success. The high rate of dancer injuries is a signpost signifying that performing arts dance training is in need of reassessment and restructuring based on the dance and sports science research.

In summary, the investigations in Chapter 2 outline current potential applications for Barre beyond a fitness regimen: for injury prevention programmes for elite athletes, classical ballet dancers, health and wellbeing initiatives; post-operative physiotherapy for elite footballers and dancers; transitioning professional performing artists to educators; and dance education in university performing arts curricula.

**Why does Barre belong in higher education performing arts curricula?**

Dance arts have a relationship with fitness conditioning as seen in the history of classical ballet and dance education. Examples include the physical rigor and sports-like repetitious training techniques seen in the Danish Bournonville style; those of renowned nineteenth-century ballerina Marie Taglioni; and the current teaching methods established by George Balanchine, known as 'the father of Neoclassical ballet'.

University dance education programmes in the United States likewise spring from the relationship between arts and sports as exemplified by the establishment of the first university-based dance programme in 1926 at the University of Wisconsin, Madison, by Margaret D'Houbler, who had a background in biology and physical education.

Chapter 3 investigates how certain fitness-based rehabilitative regimens metamorphosed into particular dance styles, for example those of Eugene Louis Facciuto ('Luigi') and Joseph Hubertus Pilates. 'Luigi', a professional dancer who was injured in a car accident, developed a system of exercises to self-rehabilitate that then became known as a jazz dance technique; and Pilates, whose exercise system developed during a four-year internment during World War I on the Isle of Man was adapted to become the foundation for Hanya Holms' contemporary dance technique. Interestingly, although Berk's programme was based on contemporary ballet, her rehabilitation programme was transformed into a popular fitness regimen that would later be called Barre. These examples suggest that the designation of programmes as fitness or art relies heavily on how they are tailored within the classroom and for the stage.

The study of shared aspects and principles of fitness and art also highlighted their differences— notably, how these programmes utilise music. In both fitness and dance, musical accompaniment is used to create an ambiance in the studio and motivate participants' performance. However, dance and the arts go even further, requiring musical accompaniment to draw forth an emotional connection that encourages individual expression and artistry, aspects that are not part of physical fitness programme intentions.

**How can the benefits claimed by Barre practitioners be investigated in academic research?**

The Crescent Arts Centre and the Physical Education Centre at Queen's University, Belfast, provided volunteers for the qualitative and quantitative investigations that are discussed in Chapters 4 and 5. Case Study 1 in Chapter 4, *Self-reported physiological and psychological effects of Barre compared with Zumba/Dance Fit*, used a questionnaire to study the effects on learners and their self-reported improvements in strength, muscle tone and control, posture, mood, and confidence as a result of participation in practises.

Overall, the study produced the following findings:

- 96% reported that attending dance-movement classes produced positive effects
- 79% reported positive changes in mood, confidence, or well-being that resulted from dance-related activity, and 87% cited a duration to the improvement

- 95% reported improved muscle strength, tone, confidence, and mood as a result of their dance-related activity
- 95% reported that the in-class musical accompaniment positively contributed to their experience

In comparative analysis of the Barre and Zumba/Dance Fit groups, the findings were similar among the groups, with a modest indication that Barre participants experienced greater physiological and psychological improvement than the participants in the Zumba/Dance Fit group.

In Chapter 5, the physiological and psychological effects on learners in Barre, Zumba, and Dance Fit programmes were expanded to explore the effects of musical accompaniment on learners. Case Study 2, *A comparison of Barre and Zumba/Dance Fit on standing leg stability and on the physiological and psychological impact of musical accompaniment on overall movement quality*, was conducted in the Movement Innovation Lab at the Physical Education Centre at Queen's University, Belfast. Using 3D Qualisy motion capture and force platform systems, participants performed a one-legged dynamic balance test to two sound conditions: with musical accompaniment, and using verbal-only cues (without music). A panel of expert evaluators from the fields of dance and sports, systems analytics, and Laban Movement Analysis (LMA) were asked to score individual participants' performances.

The three dance and sports evaluators scored the Barre and Zumba/Dance Fit groups similarly on the dynamic balance test, with the Barre group scoring marginally higher on the following technical skills:

- Strength in the supporting leg/foot
- Consistency and control in the moving leg/foot
- Coordination between hand, leg, and head movements; posture, including core engagement

The systems expert also found that participants performed similarly in the one-legged balance test regardless of group, and that participants in all groups developed better balance skills, with participants of the Barre group improving at a marginally higher rate.

The LMA analysts found that the participant-subject featured in the researcher's video documentary demonstrated physiological and psychological improvement when she performed the choreographed Barre sequence and one-legged dynamic balance test to musical accompaniment versus verbal-only cues (without music). The LMA analysts based their evaluation on the video documentary, whereas the dance/sports evaluators analysed the 3D motion capture and force platform data renderings ('dancing dots') to score participants.

The Barre participants in both case studies where novices, as Barre had only recently been introduced in Belfast, compared to the Zumba and Dance Fit participants, most of whom had several years of prior study and the opportunity to practise daily in classes offered at the Physical Education Centre. This may infer that the marginally higher scores in the Barre group may have been even better had the participants been more experienced and given equal practise opportunity.

**Does this thesis support its recommendation to integrate Barre methodology into higher education performing arts curricula?**

The fitness-conditioning and arts aspects of Barre have a historical connection to contemporary dance, classical ballet, sports, rehabilitation and injury prevention, and dance education in higher education. The researcher's doctoral advisors at Queen's University, Belfast, experts in music and psychology, offer their individual perspectives:

Dr Franziska Schroeder, Reader in the School of Arts, English and Languages, first advisor to the researcher, video-documentary *The High Barre*:

> She [the researcher] works a lot with my students, teaching them body awareness, breathing, and maybe how to think about the way they move when they're onstage . . . They might be opera singers, also very traditional musicians, and some that might be more experimental, but they all have in common that they have to go onstage and use their bodies to speak to an audience.

Dr Matthew Rodger, Senior Lecturer, School of Psychology, second advisor to the researcher, video-documentary *The High Barre*:

> I certainly hadn't engaged in the idea of dance as having the different kinds of benefits both beyond movement but also psychologically and neurologically that she's [the researcher] been able to point towards. It certainly has opened my eyes to what dance as an art form and as a mode of education can do . . . So, all of this is pointing to a story in which dance is good not just for movement but also for

motivation, for emotion, and sense of self because it has to do with the way that the brain and the body connect to each other, and they're not just distinct parts… This may allow us to infer that in the kind of Barre training that Jill has developed, what may be going on in the brain because of the complexity of the movement and the skilful nature of it, is actually more advantageous than just moving for its own sake as a kind of physical activity.

The researcher's original Barre teacher-training manual, *The High Barre: Barre for the performing arts in higher education*, and the researcher's original system for pairing practises to musical accompaniment, *The Jacobs Method of Notation*, are available at www.jillrosejacobs.com. This notation method was authored during the course of doctoral study and motivated by the research on cognition that examines the effects of dance on the brain.

*The High Barre* manual outlines best practises for tailoring specific Barre content for dance education curricula across performing arts disciplines, including for opera singers, vocal and instrumental musicians, musical theatre artists, contemporary and classical ballet dancers, actors, and others. Although some of the recommended Barre exercises may seem incongruent within the context of traditional dance practises (i.e., push-ups, upper-body strengthening exercises, extended durations of one-legged balances, cardiovascular training, alternating training of predominant muscle groups, and core strengthening exercises), these conditioning elements have been documented to improve balance, control, technique, and to enhance performance skills. The following studies provide examples that support this assertion:

- *'Association between selected physical fitness parameters and esthetic competence in contemporary dancers'*: There were significant correlations between the aesthetic competence score and jump ability and push-ups . . . analysis revealed that the best predictor of aesthetic competence was push-ups . . . analyses also revealed that the interaction of push-ups and jump ability improved the prediction power of aesthetic competence . . . It is concluded that upper body muscular endurance and jump ability best predict aesthetic competence of the present sample of contemporary dancers. (Angioi et al., 2009)

- *'The dancer as a performing athlete: Physiological considerations'*: Data on male and female ballet dancers revealed that supplemental resistance training for hamstrings and quadriceps can lead to improvements in leg strength, without interfering with key artistic and physical performance requirements. (Koutedakis & Jamurtas, 2004)

- *'Do increases in selected fitness parameters affect the aesthetic aspects of classical ballet performance?'*: In sports, fatigue has been shown to have a detrimental effect on skill... Therefore, dancers with better aerobic fitness levels will be less affected by fatigue and its deleterious effects on dance technique and performance. (Twitchett et al., 2011)

- *'Muscular imbalances and balance capability in dance'*: Research indicates that muscular imbalances between the right and left sides of the body are related to overload on the predominant side, leading to injuries to hands, wrist, triceps, and shoulders. (Wanke et al., 2018)

- 'Dance, balance and core muscle performance measures are improved following a 9-week core stabilization training program among competitive collegiate dancers': This core stabilization training program improves pirouette ability, balance (static and dynamic), and measures of muscle performance. Additionally, ADIM (abdominal draw-in maneuver) training resulted in immediate and short-term (nine-week) improvements in TrA (transversus abdominis) activation in a functional dance position. (Watson et.al., 2017)

Based on the investigations in this thesis, the researcher recommends 1) integration of Barre methodology tailored for the development of physiological conditioning to enhance the artists' on-stage capabilities and prevent injuries; 2) the incorporation of choreographed practises that mimic the action and intensity of the artists' on-stage performance; 3) choreographed practices that are repeated for a duration of time (6-8 weeks) to maximize and track participants' improvements, after which the following routine is choreographed to challenge different muscle groups (i.e., abductors/adductors) to musical accompaniment (playlist) that varies in genre, rhythm, and BPM's; and 4) to establish on-going professional training for educators that includes current information from the research in dance and sports sciences and from other fields that are relevant to dance and the performing arts in order to continually assess and hone the performing art practises in higher education.

The researcher posits that Barre is a highly adaptable methodology that can be tailored to bolster higher education performing arts curricula. The holistic nature of such a Barre programme for use in the performing arts in higher education suggests an improved trajectory for the performing artist and their well-being, in and beyond their professional career. For the university, modernising its approach to traditional performing arts curricula will not only improve outcomes for its performing arts learners but will also provide new research opportunities within the university setting that can be applied to creating impactful programmes for academia and beyond.

# Works Cited

Ackermann, B. J. & Bronner, S. (2019). Health on the Move – Challenges in Work and Lifestyle Changes for Performing Artists. *Medical Problems of Performing Artists, 34,* 169-169.

Adlerton, A.K.; Moritz, U.; & Moe-Nilssen, R. (2003). Force plate and accelerometer measures for evaluating the effect of muscle fatigue on postural control during one-legged stance. *Physiotherapy Research International, 8*(4), 187-199.

Allen, N. & Wyon, M. (2008). Dance medicine: Artist or athlete? *SportEX Medicine, 35,* 6-9.

Ambegaonkar, Jatin P.; Caswell, Shane V.; Winchester, Jason B.; Caswell, Amanda; & Andre, Matthew J. (2012). Upper-body muscular endurance in female university-level modern dancers: a pilot study. *Journal of Dance Medicine Science, 16*(1), 3-7.

Amorim, T. P.; Sousa, F.; Machado, L.; & Dos Santos, J. A. (2011). Influence of Pilates training on muscular strength and flexibility in dancers. *Motriz: Revista de Educação Física, 17*(4).

Andersen, J. C. (2005). Stretching Before and After Exercise: Effect on Muscle Soreness and Injury Risk. *Journal of Athletic Training, 40*(3), 218–220.

Angioi, M.; Metsios, G. S.; Twitchett, E.; Koutedakis, Y.; & Wyon, M. (2009). Association between selected physical fitness parameters and aesthetic competence in contemporary dancers. *Journal of Dance Medicine Science, 13*(4), 115-123.

*Association of Russian Ballet & Theatre Arts.* Hertfordshire: ARBTA.

Astrand, P. O. & Rodahl, K. (2004). *Textbook of Work Physiology: Physiological Bases of Exercise.* 4th Edition. (New York: McGraw-Hill).

Austin, Z., & Sutton, J. (2015). Qualitative research: Data collection, analysis, and management. *Can J of Hosp Pharm, 68*(3), 226-231.

Bach, L. (1973). Awake! Aware! Alive! Exercises for a Vital Body. (New York: Random House).

---. (1982). The Lotte Berk Method: Formerly Called Awake! Aware! Alive! Exercises for a Vital Body.

---. (2018-2021). Personal communication.

Berk, L. & Prince, J. (1978). The Lotte Berk Method of Exercise. (Aylesbury, Bucks: Quartet Books).

Bailey, M. (2018a). Raising the barre: How science is saving ballet dancers: Could new science and high-tech training protect dancers from the injuries that end so many of their careers far too early? The Observer.

Bailey, M. (2018b). Raising the barre: How science is saving ballet dancers: Could new science and high-tech training protect dancers from the injuries that end so many of their careers far too early? *The Guardian.*

Baldari, C. & Guidetti, L. (2001). VO2max, ventilatory and anaerobic thresholds in rhythmic gymnasts and young female dancers. *Journal of Sports Medicine and Physical Fitness, 41,* 177-182.

Beder, J. (2016). Beta-blockers, performance anxiety, and the results of the musicians' health survey. *Musician's Health Collective* (website).

Bennett, D., & Steinberg, A. (2006). Musicians as teachers: Developing a positive view through collaborative learning partnerships. *International Journal of Music Education, 24*(3), 219-230.

Bhaskaran, K.; Douglas, I.; Forbes, H.; Dos-Santos-Silva, I.; Leon, D. A.; & Smeeth, L. (2014). Body-mass index and risk of 22 specific cancers: A population-based cohort study of 5·24 million UK adults. *Lancet, 384*(9945), 755-765.

Brinck, I. (2018). Empathy, engagement, entrainment: the interaction dynamics of aesthetic experience. *Cognitive Process, 19*(2), 201-213.

Burt, J.; Wilson, R.; & Willardson, J. M. (2007). A comparison of once versus twice per week training on leg press strength in women. *Journal of Sports Medicine and Physical Fitness, 47*(1), 13-17.

Cascone, S. (2018). Art world: Fine arts majors have the worst job prospects in the US, says a new study: Their salaries are the lowest and unemployment rates the highest. *Artnet News.*

Cheshire, A. (2019-2021). Personal communication.

Clarkson, P. M. & Skriniar, M. (1988). Science in dance. *Science of Dance Training.* Champagne, IL: Human Kinetics Books. 17-21.

Cohen, J. L.; Gupta, P. K.; Lichstein, E.; & Chadda, K. D. (1980). The heart of a dancer: Noninvasive cardiac evaluation of professional ballet dancers. *American Journal of Cardiology, 45*(5), 959-965.

Cohen, J. L.; Potosnak, L.; & Frank, O. (1985). A nutritional and hematological assessment of elite ballet dancers. *The Physician and Sportsmedicine, 13*(5), 43-54.

Cohen, J. L.; Segal, K. R.; & AcArdle, W. D. (1982). Heart rate response to ballet stage performance. *The Physician and Sportsmedicine, 10*(11), 120-133.

Coldewey, D. (2016). Real-time motion capture system from Disney research uses as few sensors as possible. *TechCrunch.*

Comier, S. & Hagman, J. (1987). *Transfer of Learning.* (San Diego: Academic Press).

Connors, B. L.; Rende, R.; & Colton, T. J. (2014). Inter-rater reliability for movement pattern analysis (MPA): Measuring patterning of behaviors versus discrete behavior counts as indicators of decision-making style. *Frontiers in Psychology, 5*(605).

Crowther, T. (2017). This is the original technique that inspired your barre class. *Pop Sugar.*

Danby, S. (1984). Royal Academy of Dancing Ballet Class: An Illustrated Guide to Learning Ballet. (London: Ebury Press).

Danby, S. (1993). Royal Academy of Dancing, Step-by-Step Ballet Class: An Illustrated Guide to the Official Ballet Syllabus. (London: Ebury Press).

DeAnda, N.; Dixon, A.; & Lipinski, T. (2016). EQU Group Fitness: Gold Barre. Unpublished manuscript.

Deczynski, R. (2016). 8 benefits of barre class that will make you want to add some plies to your workout. Bustle.

Delapperall, C. (2019). Personal interview.

Dennett, D. (1991). Consciousness Explained. (New York: Penguin Books).

Descoteaux, J. (2014). Substance Use Patterns of Performing Artists: A Preliminary Study. (electronic thesis/dissertation).

DeVito, F. & Halfpapp, E. (2013). TT Barre Certified by exhale, Module 1. 13th edition.

---. (2013). TT barre certified by exhale, Module 2. 5th edition.

---. (2015). Barre Fitness: Barre Exercises You Can Do Anywhere for Flexibility, Core Strength, and a Lean Body. (Beverly, Massachusetts: Fair Winds Press).

DiFrancisco-Donoghue, J., & Werner, W. (2006). Comparison of once-weekly and twice-weekly strength training in older adults. British Journal of Sports Medicine, 41(1), 19–22.

Duberg, A. e. A. (2013). Influencing Self-rated Health Among Adolescent Girls with Dance Intervention: A Randomized Controlled Trial. Journal of the American Medical Association (JAMA) Pediatric, 167(1), 27-31.

Edwards, S. (2015). Dancing and the brain. *On The Brain* (newsletter). Harvard Medical School: Harvard Mahoney Neuroscience Institute.

Eisner, E. (1982). *Cognition and Curriculum; A Basis for Deciding What to Teach.* (New York: Longman).

---. (1994). *Cognition and curriculum reconsidered.* 2nd Edition. (New York: Teachers College Press).

Ekstrand, J.; Hagglund, M.; & Walden, M. (2011). Injury incidence and injury patterns in professional football: The UEFA injury study. *British Journal of Sport Medicine, 45*(7), 552-559.

Evans, J. W. (2019). Periodized Resistance Training for Enhancing Skeletal Muscle Hypertrophy and Strength: A Mini-Review. *Frontiers in Physiology.*

Evans, R. W.; Evans, R. I.; & Carvajal, S. (1998). Survey of injuries among west end performers. *Occupational & Environmental Medicine, 55*(9), 585-593.

Evans, R. W.; Evans, R. I.; Carvajal, S.; & Perry, S. (1996). A survey of injuries among Broadway performers. *American Journal of Public Health, 86*(1), 77-80.

Facciuto, E. L. (1987). *Danza Jazz: La tecnica di Luigi.* (Roma: Di Giacomo Editore).

Fairfax, E. & Jacobs, J. (2017). *An Interview with Esther Fairfax.* (Hungerford, Berkshire).

Fairfax, E.; Kenna, B.; & Whee, M. (2016). *The Lotte Berk Method* (Barre manual).

Fairfax, E. (1991). *Fit to Survive.* (Hungerford: Fairfax Publications).

---. (1978). *Help Yourself to Health: Exercises That Really Work for Men and Women.* (London: MacDonald and Jane's).

---. (2010). *My Improper Mother and Me.* (Hebden Bridge: Pomona Books).

---. (2014). *Lotte Berk Technique Warm-Up Exercises.* YouTube.

---. (2016). Eccentric Upbringing. *Lotte Berk's Daughter Talks* (blog).

---. (2017). Angels Do Exist. *Lotte Berk's Daughter Talks* (blog).

---. (2017). Personal communication.

Fairfax, J. (2021). Personal communication.

Feeney, M. (2017). Barre originator? Who is Lotte Berk and Why is She Considered to be a Barre Originator? *The Barre Blog*.

Finkelstein, E. A.; Trogdon, J. G.; Cohen, J. W.; & Dietz, W. (2009). Annual medical spending attributable to obesity: Payer-and service-specific estimates. *Health Affects, 28*(5), 822-831.

Friedman, D. (2018). The Secret Sexual History of the Barre Workout. The fitness phenomenon once taught women how to radically improve their sex. *New York* (Magazine).

Gardner, H. (1983). Frames of Mind: The Theory of Multiple Intelligences. (New York: Basic Books).

---. (1991). The unschooled mind: How children think and how schools should teach. (New York: Basic Books).

---. (1998). A multiplicity of intelligences. Scientific American, 9, 19-23.

Gough, C. (2021). Health & Fitness Clubs - Statistics & Facts. Statista.

Guidetti, L.; Caldari, C.; Capranica, L.; Persichini, C.; & Figura, F. (2000). Energy cost and energy sources of ball routine in rhythmic gymnastics. International Journal of Sports Medicine, 21(3), 205-209.

Guimaraes, A. C.; Vaz, M. A.; De Campos, M. I.; & Marantes, R. (1991). The contribution of the rectus abdominis and rectus femoris in twelve selected abdominal exercises. An electromyographic study. Journal of Sports Medicine and Physical Fitness, 31(2), 222-230.

Gvion, Liora. (2008). Dancing bodies, decaying bodies: The interpretation of anorexia among Israeli dancers. Sage, 15(1), 67-87.

Haldane, C. R. (2018). Balancing performing and teaching roles: The voice of classical singers. *Frontiers in Psychology, 9*, 2503.

Halfpapp, E. (2018-2021). Personal communication.

Halpern, A. (1988). Perceived and imagined tempos of familiar songs. *Music Perception: An Interdisciplinary Journal, 6*(2), 193-202.

Hamacher, D.; Schiller, F.; Rehfeld, K.; & Hockelmann, A. (2015). The effect of a six-month dancing program on motor-cognitive dual-task performance in older adults. *Journal of Aging and Physical Activity, 23*(4), 647-652.

Hanna, J. L. (1999). *Partnering Dance and Education: Intelligent Moves for Changing Times.* (Champaign, Illinois: Human Kinetics).

---. (2006). *Dancing for Health.* Revised edition. (Lanham, Maryland: AltaMira Press).

Helmar, J. (2020). Barre Classes: Benefits, Exercises, and What to Expect. *WebMD*.

Hinde, R., ed. (1972). *Non-Verbal Communication.* (New York: Cambridge University Press).

Homas, J. (2010). *Apollo's Angels*. (New York: Random House).

Hopkins, A. (2018). How the barre workout was created: German-born dancer who fled the Nazis devised an exercise regime with moves like the "love-making position" - but died in anonymity after selling the rights to her own name. *DailyMail.com*.

Hopper, L. S.; Weidemann, A. L.; & Karin, J. (2018). The inherent movement variability underlying classical ballet technique and the expertise of a dancer. *Research in Dance Education, 19*(3), 229-239.

Hu, F. B.; Li, T. Y.; Colditz, G. A.; Willett, W. C.; & Manson, J. E. (2003). Television watching and other sedentary behaviors in relation to risk of obesity and type 2 diabetes mellitus in women. *Journal of the American Medical Association (JAMA), 289*(14).

Hughes, L. (2015). WTF are Barre Workouts and are they Actually Worth Doing? *The Active Times* (blog).

Huxel Bliven, K. C. & Anderson, B. E. (2013). Core stability training for injury prevention. *Sports Health, 5*(6), 514-522.

Hymes, D. H. (1974). *Foundations on Sociolinguistics: An Ethnographic Approach*. (Philadephia, PA: University of Pennsylvania Press).

Irvine, S.; Redding, E.; & Rafferty, S. (2011). Dance Fitness (resource paper for dance teachers). *International Association for Dance Medicine & Science*.

Jacobs, J. R. & Buckley, A. (2017). *An Interview with Esther Fairfax* (video-recorded documentary). (Hungerford, Berkshire). Available at: Part 1 - https://youtu.be/JvGn6DGrJiY and Part 2 - https://www.dropbox.com/s/c7veuqt9e4axgo2/Esther%20Interview%20Part%202.mp4?dl=0

---. (2018). *Jill Rose Jacobs Dance Study* (video-recorded documentary). (Belfast: Queen's University, Movement Innovation Lab). Available at: https://youtu.be/HlBkEQ6MCNY

Jacobs, J. R.; Moloney, D.; & Murphy, P. *A Short Film by Donal Moloney, The High Barre: A PhD Journey with Jill Rose Jacobs*. (Belfast: Queen's University and Crescent Arts Centre). Available at https://youtu.be/Jiu_o68IGsE

Jardine, C. (2010). Lotte Berk: One of the strangest and most ruthless characters of the 20th Century. *The Telegraph*.

Jensen, M. & Ryan, D. (2013). Managing overweight and obesity in adults: Systematic evidence review from the obesity expert panel (evidence report).

Jones, D. A. & Round, J. M. (1990). *Skeletal Muscle in Health and Disease, a Textbook of Muscle Physiology*. (Manchester: Manchester University Press).

Karageorghis, I., & Terry, C. P. (2011). Music in sport and exercise. *The New Sport and Exercise Psychology Companion*. (Morgantown, West Virginia: Fitness Information Technology). 359-380.

Karpljuk, D.; Meško, M.; Strojnik, V.; & Videmšek, M. (2009). The effect of listening to techno music on reaction times to visual stimuli. *Acta Universitatis Palackianae Olomucensis. Gymnica, 39*(1), 67-73.

Karst, G. M. & Willett, G. M. (2004). Effects of specific exercise instructions on abdominal muscle activity during curl exercises. *Journal of Orthopedic & Sports Physical Therapy, 34*(1), 4-12.

Kasen, S.; Cohen, P.; & Chen, H. (2008). Obesity and psychopathology in women: A three decade prospective study. *International Journal of Obesity, 32*(3), 558-566.

Kattenstroth, J.; Kolankowska, I.; Kalisch, T.; & Rinse, H. R. (2010). Superior sensory, motor, and cognitive performance in elderly individuals with multi-year dancing activities. *Frontiers in Aging Neuroscience, 2,* 31.

Kenna, B. (2019). Personal communication.

Kirkland, G. (1986). *Dancing on My Grave.* (New York: Doubleday).

Kirsch, M. (2004). Leader of the Dance. *The Guardian.*

Kloberdanz, K. (2020). Actors: All the World's a Hazard. *Health Day.*

Kloubec, J. (2011). Pilates: how does it work and who needs it? *Muscle, Ligaments, and Tendons Journal, 1*(2), 61–66.

Knapik, J. J.; Jones, B. H.; Bauman, C. L.; & Harris J. M. (1992). Strength, flexibility and athletic injuries. *Sports Medicine, 14*(5), 277-288.

*Knockaloe.im* (website). (Pilates/Kockaloe/Isle of Man).

Koutedakis, Y.; Khaloula, M.; Pacy, P. J.; Murphy, M.; & Dunbar, G. M. J. (1997). Thigh peak torques and lower-body injuries in dancers. *Journal of Dance Medicine & Science, 1*(1), 12-15.

Koutedakis, Y.; Agrawal, A.; & Craig Sharp, N. C. (1999). Isokinetic characteristics of knee flexors and extensors in male dancers, Olympic oarsmen, Olympic bobsleighers, and non-athletes. *Journal of Dance Medicine & Science, 2*(2), 63-67.

Koutedakis, Y.; Stavropoulous-Kalinoglou, A.; & Metsios, G. (2005). The significance of muscular strength in dance. *Journal of Dance Medicine & Science, 9*(1), 29-34.

Koutedakis, Y.; Hukam, H.; Metrsios, G.; Nevill, A.; Giakas, G.; Jamurtas, A.; & Myszkewycz, L. (2007). The effects of three months of aerobic and strength training on selected performance and fitness-related parameters in modern dance students. *Journal of Strength and Conditioning Research, 21*(3), 808-812.

Koutedakis, Y. & Jamurtas, A. (2004). The dancer as a performing athlete: Physiological considerations. *Sports Medicine, 34*(10), 651-661.

Koutedakis, Y. & Craig Sharp, N. C. (1999). *The Fit and Healthy Dancer.* (Hoboken, NJ: Wiley).

Landoli, K. (2017). Dance music the leisure principle: Why dance music is slowing down. *The Guardian.*

Lardieri, A. (2018). High and Low BMI Linked to Increased Risk of Death. *US News & World Report.*

Laskowski, Edward R., MD. (2018). Exercise: How much do I need every day? Mayo Clinic.

Laws, H.; Parker, D.; Apps, J.; & Bramley, I. (2005). *Fit to dance 2: Report of the second national inquiry into dancers' health and injury in the UK.* (MacVean: Dance UK).

Lin, C.; Chen, S.; Su, F.; Wu, H.; & Lin, C. (2014). Differences of ballet turns (pirouette) performance between experienced and novice ballet dancers. *Research Quarterly for Exercise and Sport, 85*(3).

Lin, T. P.; Theodore, C. K. M.; Lombardi, D. A. P.; & Verma, S. K. M. (2015). Association between sedentary work and BMI in a U.S. national longitudinal survey. *Preventive Medicine, 49*(6), 117-123.

London, B. (2015). It's the Workout that Victoria's Secret Angels and Every A-Lister Swears by to Stay Toned and as Barre Launches in the UK, FEMAIL tries Hollywood's favourite exercise class. *DailyMail.com.*

London, G. A. (2015). The Cult of Barre Beware Barre Babes of Drinking the Kool-Aid. *Psychology Today.*

Madden, B. (2014). The resonant human: The science of how tempo affects us. *SonicScoop.*

MacDougall, J. D.; Elder, G. C.; Sale, D. G.; Moroz, J. R.; & Sutton, J. R. (1980). Effects of strength training and immobilization on human muscle fibres. *European Journal of Applied Physiology and Occupational Physiology, 43*(1), 25-34.

MacVean, M. (2015). Why Barre Fitness Classes are Exploding in Popularity: 'Everyone can do it'. *Los Angeles Times.*

McLeod, T. C. V.; Armstrong, T.; Miller, M.; & Sauers, J. L. (2009). Balance improvements in female high school basketball players after a 6-week neuromuscular-training program. *Journal of Sport Rehabilitation, 18*(4), 465.

Meng, X.; Li, G.; Jia, Y.; Liu, Y.; Shang, B.; Liu, P.; Bao, X.; & Chen, L. (2019). Effects of dance intervention on global cognition, executive function and memory of older adults: A meta-analysis and systematic review. *Aging Clinical and Experimental Research, 32*(1), 7-19.

Misigoj-Durakovic, M.; Matkovic, B. R.; Ruzic, L.; Durakovic, Z.; Zdravko, B.; Sasa., K.; & Ovancic-Kosuta, M. (2001). Body composition and functional abilities in terms of the quality of professional ballerinas. *Collegium Antropologicum, 25*(2), 585-590.

Morris, S. (2017). Personal communication.

Muller, P.; Rehfeld, K.; Schmicker, M.; Hokelmann, A.; Kaufmann, J.; & Muller, N. (2017). Evolution of neuroplasticity in response to physical activity in old age: The case for dancing. *Frontiers in Aging Neuroscience, 9*(56).

Muzaffar, M. (2014). 'A dancer dies twice': The unique, sad challenge of retiring from ballet. *The Atlantic.*

National Endowment for the Arts. (2019). 'Artists and Other Cultural Workers: A Statistical Portrait'.

Nord Anglia Education (website). 23 March 2020.

Ogden, C. L.; Carroll, M. D.; Kit, B. K.; & Flegal, K. M. (2012). Prevalence of obesity in the United States, 2009-2010. *NCHS (National Center for Health Statistics) Data Brief,* (82), 1-8.

Patel, A. V.; Bernstein, L.; Deka, A.; Feigelson, H. S.; Campbell, P. T.; Gapstur, S. M.; Colditz, G. A.; & Thun, M. J. (2010). Leisure time spent sitting in relation to total mortality in a prospective cohort of US adults. *American Journal of Epidemiology, 172*(4), 419-429.

Petibois, C.; Cazorla, G.; Poortmans, J.R.; & Déléris, G. (2002). Biochemical aspects of overtraining in endurance sports: A review. *Sports Medicine, 32*(13), 867-878.

Peretz, I. & Zatorre, R., eds. (2003). *The Cognitive Neuroscience of Music.* (Oxford: Oxford University Press).

Ploutz, L. L.; Tesch, P. A.; Biro, R. L.; & Dudley, G. A. (1985). Effect of resistance training on muscle use during exercise. *Journal of Applied Physiology, 76*(4), 1675-1681.

Powell, H. (2016). Fitness is fun: Barre ballet (blog).

Ralston, G. W.; Kilgore, L.; Wyatt, F. B.; & Buchan, D. (2018). Weekly training frequency effects on strength gain: A meta-analysis. *Sports Medicine, 4*(1), 36.

Rasool, J. & George, K. (2007). The impact of single-leg dynamic balance training on dynamic stability. *Physical Therapy in Sport, 8*(4), 177-184.

Redding, E.; Weller, P.; Ehrenberg, S.; Irvine, S.; Quin, E.; Rafferty, S.; Wyon, M.; & Cox, C. (2009). The development of a high intensity dance performance fitness test. *Journal of Dance Medicine & Science, 13*(1), 3-9.

Rehfeld, K.; Luders, A.; Hotelman, A.; Lessmann, V.; Kaufmann, J.; Brigadski, T.; Müller P.; & Müller N. G. (2018). Dance training is superior to repetitive physical exercise in inducing brain plasticity in the elderly. *PLOS One, 13*(7).

Rehfeld, K.; Muller, P.; Aye, N.; Schmicker, M.; Dordevic, M.; Kaufmann, J.; Hökelmann, A.; & Müller, N. G. (2017). Dancing or fitness sport? The effects of two training programs on hippocampal plasticity and balance abilities in healthy seniors. *Frontiers in Human Neuroscience, 11*, 305.

Resnick, L. B. (1989). Developing mathematical knowledge. *American Psychologist, 44*(2), 162–169.

Roberts, R. E.; Deleger, S.; Strawbridge, W. J.; & Kaplan, G. A. (2003). Prospective association between obesity and depression: Evidence from the alameda county study. *International Journal of Obesity, 27*(4), 514-521.

Rodger, Matthew. (2020). *The High Barre Film* (video-recorded documentary).

Romano, E. A. & Pont, J. (2013). *Hubertus Joseph Pilates: The Biography.*

Romer, L. M.; McConnell, A. K.; & Jones, D. A. (2002). Effects of inspiratory muscle training on time-trial performance in trained cyclists. *Journal of Sports Science, 20*(7), 547-562.

Rosenstein, N. & Newkirk-Arkin, P. (2014). *Equinox: EQU Group Fitness, Inside Out Barre, Instructor Training & Choreography* (Barre manual).

---. (2016). *Equinox: EQU Group Fitness, Barre Burn, Instructor Training & Choreography* (Barre manual).

Ross, K. (2012). *Q10 with the Physique 57 Girls* (website).

Ross, J. (2000). *Moving Lessons: Margaret H'Doubler and the Beginning of Dance in American Education.* (Madison, Wisconsin: University of Wisconsin Press).

Royal, K. A.; Farrow, D.; Mujika, I.; Halson, S.; L, Pyne, D.; & Abernathy, B. (2006). The effects of fatigue on decision making and shooting skill performance in water polo players. *Journal of Sports Science, 24*(8), 807-815.

Russell, J. A., & Daniell, B. M. (2018). Concussion in theater. *Journal of Occupational and Environmental Medicine, 60*(3), 205-210.

Sandall, E. (2018). Is it time to completely rethink ballet class? *Dance Magazine.*

Saxon, W. (2003). Lotte Berk, 90, German dancer who slimmed London's stylish. *The New York Times.*

Schoenfeld, B. J.; Ogborn, D.; & Krie, J. W. (2016). Effects of resistance training frequency on measures of muscle hypertrophy: A systematic review and meta-analysis. *Sports Medicine, 46*(11), 1689-1697.

Schroeder, F. (2020). *The High Barre Film* (video-recorded documentary).

Sebeok, T. A. & Umider-Sebeok, J., eds. (2012). *The Semiotic Sphere.* (New York: Springer).

Seidel, S. (2016). Barre workout: Can it give you a dancer's physique? *Dr. Axe* (website).

Shufelt, C. L.; Torbati, T. B.; & Dutra, E. B. (2017). Hypothalamic amenorrhea and the long-term health consequences. *Seminars in Reproductive Medicine, 35*(3), 256-262.

Sibley, B. A., & Etnier, J., L. (2003). The relationship between physical activity and cognition in children: A meta-analysis. *Pediatric Exercise Science, 15*(3), 243-256.

Sides, S. (2021). The Down and Dirty History of Barre Fitness. *GXUNITED* (blog).

Singley, M. K. & Anderson, J. R. (1989). *The Transfer of Cognitive Skill (Cognitive Science Series).* (Cambridge, MA: Harvard University Press).

Sogari, G.; Velez-Argumendo, C.; Gomez, M. I.; & Mora, C. (2018). College students and eating habits: A study using an ecological model for healthy behavior. *Nutrients, 10*(12), 1823.

Solomon, G. & Perkins, DN. (1989). Are Cognitive Skills Context-Bound? *Sage Journals, 18*(1), 16-25.

Solomon, R. & Solomon, J. (2020) *Dance Medicine and Science Bibliography.* 8th Edition.

Stalder, M. A.; Noble, B. J.; & Wilkinson, J. G. (1990). The effects of supplemental weight training for ballet dancers. *Journal of Strength and Conditioning Research, 4*(3), 95-102.

Stonnington, C. M.; Krell-Roesch, J.; & Locke, D. E. C.; Hentz, J. G; Dueck, A. C.; Geda, Y. E.; Tariot, P. N.; & Caselli, R. J. (2019). Impact of Zumba on cognition and quality of life is independent of APOE4 carrier status in cognitively unimpaired older women: A 6-month randomized controlled pilot study. *American Journal of Alzheimer's Disease & Other Dementias, 35.*

Stubbe, J. H.; van Beijsterveldt, A.M.; van der Knaap, S.; Stege, J.; Verhagen, E. A.; van Mechelen, W.; & Backx, F. J. (2015). Injuries in professional male soccer players in the Netherlands: A prospective cohort study. *Journal of Athletic Training, 50*(2), 211-216.

Suri, P.; Hunter, D. J.; Jouve, C.; Hartigan, C.; Limke, J.; Pena, E.; Swaim, B.; Li, L.; & Rainville, J. (2010). Inciting events associated with lumbar disk herniation. *Spine Journal, 10*(5), 388-395.

Tarsy, Daniel. (2015). Dancing on the Brain. *On the Brain* (website). (Harvard Medical School: Harvard Mahoney Neuroscience Institute).

Thomason, K. (2021). What is barre and is it actually a good workout?: Don't be intimidated by this fitness class. *Women's Health.*

Tindall, B. (2004). Better playing through chemistry. *The New York Times.*

Toth, P. (2018). Knowledge Building: A Process to Understanding Your Learning Process. *The Learning Exchange* (website).

Travers, Colleen. (2019). The beginner's guide to barre class: here's what you need to know before you hit the bar(re). *Shape.*

Twitchett, E. A.; Angioi, M.; Koutedakis, Y.; & Wyon, A. (2011). Do increases in selected fitness parameters affect the aesthetic aspects of classical ballet performance? *Medical Problems of Performing Artists, 26*(1), 35-38.

Videman, T.; Battie, M. C.; & Gibbons, L. E. (1997). Lifetime exercise and disk degeneration: An MRI study of monozygotic twins. *Medicine and Science in Sports and Exercise, 29*(10), 1350-1356.

Videman, T.; Kapprio, J.; & Battie, M. C. (2010). Challenging the cumulative injury model: Positive effects of greater body mass on disc degeneration. *The Spine Journal, 10*(1), 26-31.

Videman, T.; Levalahti, E.; & Battié, M. C. (2007). The effects of anthropometrics, lifting strength, and physical activities in disc degeneration. *Spine, 32*(13), 1406-1413.

Viikari-Juntura, M. H.; Martikainen, E.; & Riihimaki, T. E. (2002). Individual factors, occupational loading, and physical exercise as predictors of sciatic pain. *Spine, 27*(10), 1102-1109.

Wahlgren, K. (2020). 7 Amazing Benefits You'll Get from a Barre Workout. *Openfit* (website).

Wainwright, S. P. & Turner, B. S. (2004). Epiphanies of embodiment: Injury, identity and the balletic body. *Sage Journals, 4*(3), 331-337.

Wainwright, S. P.; Williams, C.; & Turner, B. S. (2005). Fractured identities: Injury and the balletic body. *Health (London), 9*(1), 49-66.

---. (2006). Varieties of habitus and the embodiment of ballet. *Sage Journals, 6*(4), 535-558.

---. (2007). Globalization, habitus, and the balletic body. *Cultural Studies – Critical Methodologies, Sage Journals, 7*(3), 308-325.

Wanke, E. M.; Schreiter, J.; Groneburg, D. A.; & Weisser, B. (2018). Muscular imbalances and balance capability in dance. *Journal of Occupational Medicine and Toxicology, 13*(36).

Watson, T.; McPherson, S.; Carter, E.; Edwards, J.; Melcher, I.; & Burgess, T. (2017). Dance, balance and core muscle performance measures are improved following a 9-week core stabilization training program among competitive collegiate dancers. *International Journal of Sports Physical Therapy, 12*(1), 25-41.

Welch, J. (2003). Obituaries: Lotte Berk: Stylish Dancer Who Became a Fitness Icon. *The Guardian.*

Werner, J.; Hägglund, M.; Waldén, M.; & Ekstrand, J. (2009). UEFA injury study: A prospective study of hip and groin injuries in professional football over seven consecutive seasons. *British Journal of Sports Medicine, 43*(13), 1036-1040.

Werner, M. J. (1991). An Overview of Health Issues for Performing and Visual Arts Students (briefing paper). *Council of Arts Accrediting Associations.*

Wernick, R. (12 February 1962). To Keep in Shape: Act Like an Animal. *Sports Illustrated.*

Willard, V. & Lavallee, D. (2016). Retirement experiences of elite ballet dancers: Impact of self-identity and social support. *Sport, Exercise, and Performance Psychology, 5*(3), 266-279.

Williams, L. (2018). What is barre class, and are barre workouts effective? *Verywellfit* (website).

Wolfgang, A. (1984). *Nonverbal Behavior: Perspectives, Applications, Intercultural Insights.* (Lewiston, NY: C.J. Hogrefe).

Wyon, M. (2007). Testing the aesthetic athlete: Contemporary dance and classical ballet dancers. *Sport and Exercise Physiology Testing Guidelines.* (London: Routledge).

Wyon, M.; Deighan, M. A.; Nevill, A. M.; Doherty, M.; Morrison, S. L.; Allen, N.; Jobson S. J.; & George, S. (2007). The cardiorespiratory, anthropometric, and performance characteristics of an international/national touring ballet company. *Journal of Strength and Conditioning Research, 21*(2), 389-393.

Wyon, M. (2010). Stretching for dance. *The International Association for Dance Medicine & Science: The IADMS Bulletin for Teachers, 2*(1), 9-12.

Wyon, M. A.; Abt, G.; Redding, E.; Head, A.; Sharp, N. C. (2004). Oxygen uptake during modern dance class, rehearsal, and performance. *Journal of Strength and Conditioning Research, 18*(3), 646-649.

Wyon, M. A. & Redding, E. (2005). The physiological monitoring of cardiorespiratory adaptations during rehearsal and performance of contemporary dance. *Journal of Strength and Conditioning Research, 19*(3), 611-614.

Yaffe, S. (2017). Abusive mum and alcoholic husband contribute to the story of Esther. *A Jewish Telegraph Newspaper.*

York-Pryce, S. (2014). *Ageism and the mature dancer* (thesis). Griffith University, Queensland College of Art, Queensland, Australia.

Zagyvane, S. I. (2017). What makes a good teacher? *Universal Journal of Educational Research, 5*(1), 141-147.

# Appendices

## Appendix A – Lotte Berk Method Registration for the United States, 2004

# LOTTE BERK METHOD

| | |
|---|---|
| Word Mark | **LOTTE BERK** METHOD |
| Goods and Services | IC 041. US 100 101 107. G & S: providing consultation and instruction in the field of physical exercise; providing fitness and exercise facilities. FIRST USE: 19710000. FIRST USE IN COMMERCE: 19710000 |
| Standard Characters Claimed | |
| Mark Drawing Code | (4) STANDARD CHARACTER MARK |
| Serial Number | 76602845 |
| Filing Date | July 19, 2004 |
| Current Basis | 1A |
| Original Filing Basis | 1A |
| Published for Opposition | September 20, 2005 |
| Registration Number | 3025691 |
| Registration Date | December 13, 2005 |
| Owner | (REGISTRANT) The Lotte Berk Method Limited CORPORATION NEW YORK 7 Muchmore Lane East Hampton NEW YORK 11937 |
| Attorney of Record | Gloria Tsui-Yip |
| Disclaimer | NO CLAIM IS MADE TO THE EXCLUSIVE RIGHT TO USE "METHOD" APART FROM THE MARK AS SHOWN |
| Type of Mark | SERVICE MARK |
| Register | PRINCIPAL |
| Affidavit Text | SECT 15. SECT 8 (6-YR). SECTION 8(10-YR) 20160201. |
| Renewal | 1ST RENEWAL 20160201 |
| Other Data | The name(s), portrait(s), and/or signature(s) shown in the mark does not identify a particular living individual. |
| Live/Dead Indicator | LIVE |

97

**Appendix B – The Lotte Berk Method Registration in the United Kingdom, 2019**

TRADE MARKS REGISTRY

REGISTRATION CERTIFICATE

Trade Marks Act 1994 of

Great Britain and Northern Ireland

I certify that the mark shown below has been registered under No. UK00003341938 effective as of the date 28/09/2018 and has been entered in the register on 14/06/2019

Signed this day at my direction

Tim Moss
REGISTRAR

Representation of Mark
THE LOTTE BERK METHOD

The mark has been registered in respect of:
Class 41:
Fitness and exercise instruction and teaching; Physical fitness consultation; Physical fitness tuition;
Conducting fitness classes; Personal and physical fitness training services; Health education;
Education services relating to fitness and exercise; Providing fitness and exercise facilities; Provision of instruction courses relating to health and fitness;
Conducting training sessions on physical fitness online; Provision of information on fitness training via an online portal; Advisory and consultancy services relating to all the aforesaid services.

In the name of Jill Jacobs

Intellectual Property Office is an operating name of the Patent Office

## Appendix C – Questionnaire

This questionnaire is for use by Jill Rose Jacobs for the sole purpose of a study to be completed at Queen's University in fulfillment of her doctoral requirements.

Dear participant,

This study aims to determine and measure possible benefits of dance-movement on the physical body and mind. Your participation in this study will provide information in the field of dance-movement education. I am the only person that will have access to your research data. Your information will be kept confidential and stored in a secure place accessible only by me. It is the policy of Queen's University to destroy all research data five years from completion of the study, envisaged to be completed by 2019.

You will have the right to withdraw from interviews at any time or at any point during the study. You may also refuse answering any question(s) that you do wish to respond to. Furthermore, should you decide upon completion of the study that you don't want your material used, for any reason, you may complete the statement at the end of this questionnaire. You will also advise me if you would like your name credited in affiliation with this study or if you prefer to remain anonymous.

Please contact me at any time by e mail: jillrosejacobs@aol.com. Thank you in advance for your contribution!

Best regards,
Jill R. Jacobs

**Dance Movement Questionnaire** (please note: spacing has been condensed)

Name: _____     Age: _____

Height (cm): _____     Weight (kg): _____

Gender: _____

Measurements (cm):   You may leave this section blank or ask for my assistance.

Chest _____     Waist _____     Hips _____     Thighs _____

Calves _____     Upper Arm _____     % of Body Fat _____

Why do you participate in a dance-movement classes/courses?

What are your other hobbies?

What is your fitness regimen (per week / day)?

Are you on a diet or making changes to your nutritional habits? Please detail what these changes are, if you are making changes.

Are these changes in your nutrition for weight gain/loss or other reasons?

What is your background in dance or sports?

Do you have injuries, health issues, or suffer from aches and pains?

Are you under a doctor's care for any condition?


TO BE COMPLETED MID STUDY

Why do you take dance-movement classes?

What do you like about your dance-movement class?

What could be better (i.e. the exercises, movements, or music) and why?

Have you noticed changes in your body? And if so, can you detail these?

Are the exercises getting easier to do, harder, or no different?

Has your mood or general well-ness changed? And if so how?

Have other people commented on changes on you, and if so, what have they said?

How do you feel during the class?

Do you feel different after dance-movement class and for how long?

Are your muscles sore following the class? Where are they sore?  How long does this soreness usually last?


TO BE COMPLETED AT THE END OF THE STUDY

Did the class help you achieve your goal(s) or the reason(s) you enrolled?

Do you feel more or less in control of your body, or no different?

Do you feel that you had physical changes as a result of your dance-movement class (i.e. posture, strength, movement, muscles, less / more pain, etc.)?

Did you have psychological changes (i.e. mood, confidence, general wellness, less/more fatigue, etc.)?

Did the music make the class easier, harder or no different (please explain)?

Did the music make the class more pleasurable, less pleasurable or have no effect? (Please explain)

Did the music have any (positive or negative) effect on challenging exercise sequences?

Do you have comments and/or suggestions?


Signature _____ Date _____

You made it! Thank you for completing the questionnaire. Your participation is greatly appreciated.

If you wish to withdraw from the research, please complete the form below and return to me at my e mail address: jillrosejacobs@aol.com. Thank you.


**PLEASE WITHDRAW ME FROM THIS STUDY.**

Signature: _____

Printed Name: _____ Date: _____

## Appendix D – Consent Form

# CONSENT FORM

### THE EFFECTS OF PRACTICE IN THE LEARNING AND FLEXIBLE USE OF A MOTOR SKILL IN A MUSICAL CONTEXT

*Please initial the statements below as appropriate*

| | | Initials |
|---|---|---|
| 1. | I agree to participate in this research | _____ |
| 2. | This agreement is completed of my own free will | _____ |
| 3. | I have been given information regarding the aims of the research and have been provided with the researchers' name(s) and contact details | _____ |
| 4. | I am aware that I may contact the researchers at any point should I require further information/assistance | _____ |
| 5. | I have been given the opportunity to ask any questions I may have about the study | _____ |
| 6. | I am aware that I have the right to withdraw from the study at any time and that I am not required to provide a reason to do so. I am also aware that should I do this, I will incur no adverse consequences | _____ |
| 7. | I am aware that even after participating, I may still request that my information is withdrawn from the study within the time period specified on the Participant Information Sheet | _____ |

PARTICIPANT

Signed:

Full Name (printed):

Date:

_____

RESEARCHER

Signed:

Full Name (printed):

Date:

_____

**Appendix E – Human Beingness observed as Expressivity through Analysis of Non-Verbal Barre Sequences**

Laban Movement Analysis (LMA) is a system for movement observation, description and recording. The analysis covers only the movement that is actually seen; not imagined. This can be notated, described and measured within a theoretical framework by trained movement observers. In research, inter-observer reliability has been confirmed at significant levels. (see Martha Davis, Pamela Ramsden; see Appendix for introduction to the LMA framework.)

Observer A was tasked to look at two excerpts of filmed barre sequences. They are ostensibly the same exercise but one is with musical accompaniment and one not. The question was; Is there any difference between the two sequences? The two observers' conclusions were that the movement done with musical accompaniment showed a more humanly expressive quality than the unaccompanied filmed segment which appeared more mechanical and less engaged.

Various filmed sequences were watched and 35 seconds were selected to observe, describe and notate. Of these 35 seconds, 18 had musical accompaniment, 15 did not. Unfortunately, this kind of movement observation needs the whole body to be visible, preferably from a front, slightly diagonal place in relation to the mover throughout the observation period. As this filming was not done for non-verbal observation procedures, we only had a limited time of un-interrupted visual material to observe.

The first of these sequences is 12 seconds of a leg lift sequence repeated twice called "higher, lower, lower, lower". It is done with verbal direction from the teacher and video recorded from behind the mover. The second event of 17 seconds is the same sequence done four times but recorded from the front of the mover and with music accompanying it. The observers did not have sound on during the analysis though they did know only the second series was accompanied by music.

Two experts in the field of Laban Movement Analysis (LMA) looked at these excerpts and wrote their observations. Observer A was given the research question about musical accompaniment and asked to note any differences between the two sequences; Observer B was asked to observe and notate Effort Phrasing used by the mover.

The observers did not look at the technical expertise of the mover – how accurate her placement or alignment is, for instance. Rather the qualitative aspect of the movement was observed. Observer A looked at Body and Shape categories while observer B observed Effort Phrasing.

**First Sequence: 4:17 – 4:29**
**Observer A:**

There is little sequencing through the body to the lifting of the arm: the "connection" between limb and torso is limited to the shoulder. There is little postural support for the movement and she uses low intensity variations of flow and time throughout. This lack of variety and intensity of dynamics, along with the lack of 'connection' and 'integration' of the torso with the arm movement gives an impression of a slightly mechanical movement: the arm moves from the shoulder, not the whole body and the dynamics are muted – all giving an impression of 'following the teacher' in the movement rather than enjoying and engaging with it on her own terms.

**Observer B:**

Only the left arm, as a separate limb, was notated – possibly indicating the segmented quality of the body's movement. Predominantly two symbols (Flow and Time), at varying degrees of lessened intensity, were used; while Lightness was only notated twice. Only one effort phrase was notated in the arm's "cycle".

**Second Sequence: 7:47 – 8:04**
**Observer A:**

Here we see the whole body involved in the movement phrase rather than just an arm moving on the torso. She begins the movement with a three-dimensional twist of her upper body that ends in the arm going up then descending while the torso continues to have Shape Flow and Postural Support for the arm's movement. Simultaneously, the head tilts forward to one side then the other; moving with an independent but integrated bobbing motion. Many more body parts are involved in an organised, flowing and three-dimensional sequence.

The phrasing and movement qualities are repeated almost exactly with each repetition: She begins the sequence with a quick free light start – almost a flick – throwing her arm up initiated by the slight twist in her upper body as if throwing the arm into the air. When the arm

104

comes down it is bound and light with a sustained quality. The phrasing style and the efforts used are similar to those of the first sequence but the intensity is greater and the sense of the body moving as an orchestrated 'whole' gives the viewer a sense of seeing someone who is engaged with the movement and enjoying themselves rather than trying to follow the instructor and 'get it right'.

Her torso has a shape flow quality that adds to an impression of enjoyment and "aliveness" to this series that was absent in the earlier filmed sequences.

**Observer B:**

The same arm movement was observed to have two phrases rather than just one. The symbol for diminished Lightness appears five times in the two-phrase pattern rather than only twice in one phrase: i.e., less dynamic 'colour' in the longer, more monotonous phrase in the first excerpt. The increased torso and head movement is also noted though not in as much detail as by the first observer as that Body level observation was not the focus.

**Points for discussion:**

The organised phrasing (two phrases instead of one) of the second series of this movement event; the added shape flow and postural support of the movement going through the torso to the arm cycle and lastly, the three-dimensional upper body movements (including the head) gives it a much more expressive, human feeling than the first one. or clearly phrased efforts. Her engagement and enjoyment of the second 'round' is confirmed by her facial expression at the start (7:46) and is much more interesting to watch.

There are more body parts moving – e.g. the head – in an integrated, phrased way: the head is like an involved commentary at the beginning and into each phrase. We are watching a pleasant conversation between different body parts in the second excerpt. In the first we are watching a student attempting to 'follow the teacher' and 'get it right' which results in a more mechanical, less human and individual expression of herself.

It may be that observing her from the back added to this impression but the difference in effort qualities and body effort and shape flow qualities are observable from the back as well as the front (e.g., the lack of a sense of "connection" or breath going through the torso into the arm in the first two sequences while there is a sense of movement – or 'flow' both in the shape and in the aliveness of the body in the second excerpt in all four leg lifts.)

**Proving "human beingness":**

We have taken "expressivity" as a core concept to support the hypothesis that musical accompaniment has enabled a more alive, human engagement with this exercise. Robots and machines are not expressive (except in Pixar and Disney films). Here, using LMA, "human being-ness" is defined as expressivity which in turn is identified through observable, notated qualities of movement which the subject's movement has when performed by her.

It would have been better to have not given the LMA observers the information about when there was music and when there was not but their observations were done with all sound turned off. Facial expression and verbal behaviour was also not observed and notated as part of the movement sequence.

**Additional notes:**

The LMA system observes and notates individual movement style and body actions. (see Appendix.) The emphasis in the observations below is on the movement patterns and phrasing that appears: body action, quality of shape flow through the torso and spatial use of limb (arm) is also used to identify differences between the two film segments and sometimes between each repetition of the leg raise. (Another aspect of human being ness: it is almost impossible, even for trained dances, to repeat a movement in exactly the same qualitative way) Every human being has his/her own phrasing preferences so observing these patterns is another way to establish difference and – in many instances – emotional expression. If there are no movement qualities – in shape or dynamics – there will be a mechanical quality that takes away any human or expressive feeling to the movement.

**Author Bio**

Dr Jill Rose Jacobs has recently completed her doctoral programme at Queen's University, Belfast, Northern Ireland, having accepted a faculty award from the School of Arts, English and Languages for academic achievement. To support Jill's research for her original programme, *The High Barre*, she received a £35,000 award from ICURe (Innovation to Commercialism of University Research) on behalf of the universities of Bath, Bristol, Exeter, Southampton, Surrey, and Queen's University, Belfast.

Prior to entering the doctoral programme, Jill was a professor for dance-movement in the department of Performing Arts Professions at New York University (NYU). She holds a master's degree from NYU in dance education and was awarded academic scholarships throughout her study. Her students are currently performers on Broadway and in musicals and operas across the country and abroad, and many are Barre instructors for leading fitness corporations. Prior to relocating to Belfast, Jill was also a Group Fitness Instructor with Equinox, where she specialized in and launched Barre programmes.

Jill's doctoral thesis, *The High Barre: An investigation of Barre for the performing arts in higher education*, posits that Barre is a highly adaptable methodology that can be tailored to bolster higher education performing arts curricula. Her research suggests that the holistic nature of such a Barre programme would improve the trajectory for the performing artist's well-being beyond their professional career. Jill's research interests include other applications for Barre methodology that feature elements of movement, music, and choreography that studies find are beneficial to participants. Her philosophy is that dance-movement is universal and that Barre methodology and practises foster improvement in muscle strength, tone, control, posture, mood, confidence, proprioception, and individualized artistic expression.

Printed in Great Britain
by Amazon

81168624R00076